RV Boondocking Basics
A Guide to Living Without Hookups

Russ and Tiña De Maris

ICanRV Publishing
Olympia, Washington

Copyright © 2003, 2004 by Russ and Tiña De Maris

All rights reserved. No part of this publication may be reproduced, stored in a retrieval system, or transmitted in any form or by any means, electronic, mechanical, photocopying, recording, or otherwise, without permission in writing from the publisher, except by a reviewer who may quote brief passages in a review.

De Maris, Russ and Tiña
    RV Boondocking Basics: A Guide to Living Without Hookups / by Russ and Tiña De Maris
    p. cm.
    Includes index
Cover photo © Russ and Tiña De Maris.

Library of Congress Control Number: 2004091467
ISBN Number: 0-9753249-0-X
Printed in the United States of America

The authors gratefully acknowledge Zack Collins, Ken Cox, and Thom Taylor for their production support.

The installation, operation, and maintenance of any RV system entails an element of risk. Always consult your system designer, the manufacturer, or supplier of your components, all applicable building, vehicle, electrical codes, and all relevant regulatory agencies before upgrading or troubleshooting your recreational vehicle. When in doubt, seek professional advice. The authors, publisher, and distributor to this work assume no liability for personal injury, property damage, or loss from using the information in this book. It is the reader/user's responsibility to exercise prudence and good judgment and to take any necessary precautions when using the methods and products described herein.

ICanRV Publishing
1910 E. 4th #119
Olympia, WA 98506
www.icanrv.com

To

Our Mothers

Ruby and Virginia

for Their Encouragement

Table of Contents

Introduction 8

Chapter 1
"We Need More Power!" 10
    Amps--A Measure of Power Usage 10
    "Shore Power" Equipment Power Usage 13

Chapter 2
Batteries--Your Electrical "Bank Account" 17
    Differences in House and SLI Batteries 18
    Sizing Batteries to Fit Your Needs 19
    Putting it All Together 20
    Types of Deep Cycle Batteries 21
    The Golf Cart "Solution" 24
    Battery Buying Decisions 25
    Hook 'em Up 26
    Parallel Wiring 26
    Series Wiring 27
    Series-Parallel Wiring 27
    Keep Your Batteries Alive 28

Battery State of Charge 29

Chapter 3
Solar: Let Sol Make Your Power 35
    Types of Solar Panels 35
    Sizing Your System 36
    Tilting Panels 27
    Solar Panel Tilt System 39
    Solar Panel Regulation 41
    Solar Installation 42
    Solar Maintenance 43

Chapter 4
Turbines--
The Answer's Blowin' in the Wind 44
    A Wind Power Disadvantage 45
    Sizing and Selection 46
    Towers 51
    Installation 53
    Operation and Maintenance 54

Chapter 5
Inverters: Shore Power--To Go 56
    Inverter Selection 56
    Power Consumption and Battery Bank 58
    Inverter Installation 59

Chapter 6
Fresh Water Wizardry 61
    Roll Out the Barrel 61
    Other Water Toters 63

Chapter 7
Don't Let Waste Water
Get You Down in the Dumps 64
- *Blue Boy Varieties 65*
- *Using Blue Boys 65*
- *Blue Boy Modifications 67*
- *Rip and Tear? Repair! 68*
- *Don't Wait--Macerate 69*
- *Odor Problems 71*

Chapter 8
Staying Warm Without Losing Your Cool 73
- *Furnace Follies 73*
- *"Cat" Heaters 74*
- *Freestanding Flame Heaters 77*
- *"Brick" Heaters 78*
- *Heater Plumbing 78*
- *Other Stay Warm Tricks 78*

Chapter 9
On the Other Hand: Hot Ideas for Staying Cool 80
- *Make Your Shade 80*
- *Mechanical Marvels 81*

Chapter 10
Boondockers' Conservation Tips 82
- *Kitchen and Bath 82*
- *And Those Clothes 84*
- *More Power to You 85*
- *Hot and Cold Running People? 86*

Appendix 87

Index 89

Introduction
The Boondocking Mindset

As your Depression Era pappy used to say, "We ain't livin' high on the hog." For the boondocker, this maxim is true. While to a degree we can extend just how much we can have, there are practical limits. The life of a boondocker doesn't have to be the life of an esthetic, but it isn't the life of a prodigal. We prefer to think of it as a conservative, yet full lifestyle.

Can you watch television? Take a shower? Vacuum the carpet? Keep warm? Yes, of course! You may choose to limit your television to a few hours a day. After hauling water in and out, you may find a short shower just as refreshing as those "drain the tank" varieties that those with utility hookups take for granted. That self-propelled gargantuan "Suck-O-Matic Vac" may give way to a smaller machine, but it'll probably be lighter and easier to manage. And yes, you won't freeze by the heat given off by a catalytic heater.

Every winter, we leave the cold and damp rain of the Pacific Northwest for the dry warmth of the Arizona desert. While hundreds of our fellow RVers are laying out hard-earned cash to stay on at area RV parks, listening to the snores of their neighbors, we don't. Instead, we head out on the desert where there's plenty of wide-open space, and the rent? We pay less to "Uncle Sam" to stay put for six months than most of the 'RV parkers' pay their landlords for two weeks in the city.

Do we give up the 'good things,' of RV park living? Not at all. We watch our television shows, keep the chill off at night, take showers, run the computer, the stereo, and microwave oven. Between the sun and the wind, our batteries are kept full, and we don't pay 17 cents a kilowatt hour for electricity. Nobody breaths down our neck when we sit by the campfire at night. Try roasting a few marshmallows in your friendly neighborhood RV park!

It's true, a little more effort is required to send out the waste water. We don't have a stadium-sized home-theater system. Still, we're content with the lifestyle that means freedom from crowds, noise, and high prices. And if ever we don't like the neighborhood, we can simply crank down the wind turbine, hitch up, and we're off to new places.

Folks ask us, "How hard is it to do this?" "How costly is it to switch to solar or wind power?" "Can anybody do this?" That's why this book was published--to show just how to make the transition from slavery to shore-based utilities and all that goes along with them, to the freedom of greater self-containment.

In short, the boondocking lifestyle means adopting a new mindset. Conservation is the key, learning to get a long with less will set you free.

Chapter 1
"We Need More Power!"

Pity Chief Engineer Scott of the Starship *Enterprise*. Captain Kirk constantly demanded, "Scotty, we need more power!" How much power does the boondocker need? There's no set rule--every boondocker's needs are different. How do you figure out your own? In this chapter we'll take a tour of your RV focussing on your equipment. Using charts and worksheets, we'll help you take note the number and types of all battery voltage consuming equipment.

After gathering the raw information, we'll show you how to chart just how much power you typically use in a day. Using that information, we'll figure out some important facts. For example, how can you produce that power? How can you store that precious commodity for later use? Get out your pencil and we'll get started.

Amps--A Measure of Power Usage

First, let's talk about power use. Every electrical device on your RV uses a given amount of electricity to perform its task. RVers measure electrical use in a unit called an amp. Amps measure the flow of electrical current, and the more power you use, the greater the amount of current flow, or amps.

For example, if you turn on the typical RV light fixture, that little bulb will consume about one and a half amps for every hour it operates. Turn on a second bulb for more light, you'll be consuming three amps for every hour the lights are on. The same is true for every other piece of electrical equipment. Turn on the water pump to take a shower, and 5 amps of electricity is used every hour that the pump runs.

The first step toward freedom from shore based utilities is knowing just *how much* power you use. To that end, we've included a worksheet that will help you determine that all-important information. Your own worksheet appears on page 16. To help you see how it's used, here's a partial "sample" worksheet.

Sample Power Consumption Worksheet

List each electricity consuming device in your RV, and estimate how many hours per day it's used. If the use is less than an hour per day, then use decimals (see chart below).

Device	How Many ??	Amp Use each device	Hours used per day	Total amp hours per day
Light, 1141	2	x 1.5	x 3	= 9
Water Pump	1	x 5.0	x .75	= 3.75
Color TV	1	x 6.0	x 3.5	= 21

```
Additional amp hours from
     inverter use  ----------------    10.5
Total daily amp hours required         44.25
```

Sample Power Consumption Worksheet, figure 1-1

The first question that comes up is, "How do I know how much 'amp use' there is for my own set of electrical gadgets?" The current consumption chart on page 15 gives a list of the most common RV 'power users.'

You may want to make photocopies of the blank "Power Consumption Worksheet." Take a copy of the worksheet and the current consumption chart, and walk through your rig. First, identify each electrical item on board. You'll find the current consumption (as expressed in amps) listed on the right side of the chart. Try to estimate as closely as you can how much time you use each device, breaking it down into hours and minutes in decimal form. To help, we show minutes to decimal conversions on the bottom of the worksheet.

When you have the worksheet filled in, you get to work the math. For each device listed, multiply the number of devices times the amp-hour use, and then by the number of per day you'll use it. Next, add up the current draw for all items and the result is the amp-hour consumption for your RV.

If any of the equipment you use doesn't appear in the chart, check the manufacturer's plate for current (or amps) used.[1] This plate is typically located on the back or bottom of the device.

The resulting calculations are expressed as "amp-hours." Every battery has its amp-hour capacity, that is, how much useful power it can provide. Likewise, you'll need amp-hour information when you determine how to recharge your RV batteries. We'll come back to that topic a little later.

---

[1] If the plate doesn't show amps, but rather watts, divide the number of watts by 12 (for 12 volts) to determine the number of amps the device consumes.

"Shore Power" Equipment Power Usage

A boondocker doesn't need to give up his use of "shore power" equipment. From microwave ovens to curling irons, with enough power and a properly sized *inverter* (a device that converts battery power to "line" voltage), you can power up most anything you'll want to use. Of course, that power has to come from somewhere. For now, let's figure up your power needs for shore power equipment.

Figuring amp-hour demands for shore power equipment is a little more complicated. First, survey your 120 volt equipment, taking note of each device's power consumption (in watts). If the manufacturer shows amps, rather than watts, then multiply the number of amps times 120 (for 120 volts). Now multiply the number of watts for each piece of equipment times the number of hours it will be used each day. Add up the resulting totals to determine daily watt-hours.

To convert watt-hours to the amp-hour requirement, divide the number of watt-hours by 12 (for 12 volts). The result now must be *multiplied by a factor of 1.2* because a power inverter is not a completely efficient device. The result of all of this is the daily amp-hour load created by your power inverter. This must be added to your daily amp-hour demand that you determined for your 12-volt equipment.

Let's say your color television will only operate on shore power. The TV operates on 120 volts, and uses 69 watts. Your "use time" is 4 hours daily. Four hours times 69 watts, gives you a daily power consumption rate of 276 watt-hours. If this were the only piece of equipment you operated with your inverter, your additional amp-hour demand would work out this way:

13

276 watt-hours divided by 12 = 23 amp-hours

23 amp-hours times 1.2 (efficiency loss) = 27.6 amp-hours additional power consumption due to inverter use.

Of course, you probably have other shore power equipment you'll want to operate using your inverter. So for the sake of calculations, take the time to calculate amp-hour demand for each of those items. Then add up the totals as "inverter amp-hour demand." We'll move that figure to the worksheet.

Where do we go with this new-found information? We'll tackle that in our next chapter.

Current Consumption Chart

Light, Incandescent, single 1141 bulb	1.5
Light, Incandescent, double 1141 bulb	2.5
Light, Incandescent, single 1003 bulb	0.9
Light, Incandescent, double 1003 bulb	1.8
Light, Fluorescent, single 8 watt tube	0.7
Light, Fluorescent, single 15 watt tube	1.2
Light, Fluorescent, double 15 watt tube	2.0
Radio/Stereo Cassette/CD Player (each)	2.0 - 5.0
Furnace Fan	2.0 - 7.0
Water Pump	3.0 - 6.0
Vent Fan, Single Speed	2.0
TV, DC Operated (color sets higher than black and white models)	1.0 - 4.0
CB Radio (receive mode)	0.5
Refrigerator, 3-way (on 12 volt mode)	10 - 35
Refrigerator (12 volt compressor type)	6.0
Swamp Cooler (12 volt)	4.5 - 20
Electric Space Heater (12 volt)	15 - 25

Power Consumption Worksheet

List each electricity consuming device in your RV, and estimate how many hours per day it's used. If the use is less than an hour per day, then use decimals (see chart below).

Device	How Many ??	Amp Use each device	Hours used per day	Total amp hours per day
_____	___ x	_____ x	_____ =	_____
_____	___ x	_____ x	_____ =	_____
_____	___ x	_____ x	_____ =	_____
_____	___ x	_____ x	_____ =	_____
_____	___ x	_____ x	_____ =	_____
_____	___ x	_____ x	_____ =	_____
_____	___ x	_____ x	_____ =	_____
_____	___ x	_____ x	_____ =	_____
_____	___ x	_____ x	_____ =	_____
_____	___ x	_____ x	_____ =	_____
_____	___ x	_____ x	_____ =	_____
_____	___ x	_____ x	_____ =	_____
_____	___ x	_____ x	_____ =	_____
_____	___ x	_____ x	_____ =	_____
_____	___ x	_____ x	_____ =	_____
_____	___ x	_____ x	_____ =	_____
_____	___ x	_____ x	_____ =	_____
_____	___ x	_____ x	_____ =	_____
_____	___ x	_____ x	_____ =	_____

Additional amp hours from
    inverter use ----------------   _____

Total daily amp hours required   _____

Decimal Equivalents

Minutes	Decimal	Minutes	Decimal
5	.08	10	.16
15	.25	20	.33
30	.5	45	.75

Chapter 2
Batteries: Your Electrical "Bank Account"

Now that you have a handle on your daily power consumption (as expressed in amp-hours), you'll want to have that power on hand for use. Power in the batteries is like money in the bank Your batteries are your electrical "bank account."

If you have a motorhome, you probably have two types of batteries on your rig: The first is the automotive or "SLI" battery, (*starting, lighting, ignition*) battery that handles the motive part of your rig. A second battery (or batteries) is the "house" or "coach" battery. House batteries take care of interior rig lighting, water pump, stereo, inverter, and other battery powered RV options. For those of us who tow our RVs, we only have house batteries in our rigs.

At one time we had an RV that drew its power from the SLI battery--it was a small truck camper that mounted on an "import" sized pickup. Our first trip out with the new RV was on a frosty-cold night. We were new to RVing, and ran the furnace all night to keep warm. Next morning, we discovered that the camper drew its power right off the truck battery, and we spent an enjoyable morning going campsite to campsite with jumper cables.

We soon added a house battery to our camper to avoid such "fun" in the future!

Differences in House and SLI batteries.

SLI batteries are called on to deliver large amounts of current for a short period of time, any time when turning over the engine to start. Several hundred amps might be summoned for a few seconds. However, as soon as the engine starts, the battery is quickly recharged by the vehicle charging system. On the other hand, house batteries are asked to deliver much smaller amounts of current, but this over a much longer time period. Different battery construction is needed to make these batteries survive their assignment.

Cut open a typical 12 or 6 volt battery and you'll find (among other things) a series of metal plates suspended in an acid solution. The plates are perforated in a grill-like pattern to allow them maximum surface contact with the acid solution. Insulating plates keep these plates separated from one another, to prevent short-circuiting.

The plates in an SLI battery are quite thin, which allows for the fast production of high amounts of current needed for engine starting. Alas, this thinness makes an SLI battery plate highly susceptible to damage if deeply discharged. "Draw down" an SLI battery very far from a full charge a few times and the battery will not recover.

House (or "deep cycle" batteries as they're called in the battery trade) are constructed with much thicker plates, which allows for deeply discharging and recharging many times--into hundreds of discharge and recharge cycles. These are clearly designated as deep cycle or "marine" batteries. Generally speaking, SLI batteries and house batteries are not interchangeable.

Sizing Batteries to Fit Your Needs

The key to sizing your house battery "bank" is in knowing your power consumption. If you haven't already calculated your daily power consumption using the worksheet and charts in Chapter 1, you'll want to do so before shopping for batteries.

A simple rule of thumb applies to battery selection for boondocking: Your battery capacity should be *at least twice as great* as your daily amp-hour demand. Why? Because the more deeply a battery is drawn down--discharged--the sooner it will wear out. A deep cycle battery should never be discharged by more than half its capacity.

This begs the question: How do you know the capacity of a given battery? A stroll along the battery aisle at the auto parts store leaves most folks with their heads swimming. CCA, MCA, Reserve Capacity, Peak Capacity--all those terms and letters (often bearing little standardization)--makes it difficult for RVers to pick out what they need. So, a glossary of battery terms:

CCA or "cold cranking amps" is a measure of the maximum number of amps that can be delivered in 30 seconds at 0 degrees Fahrenheit. This is a good measure for comparing SLI batteries, but useless for comparing house batteries.

MCA or "marine cranking amps" is similar to CCA, only here the standard is how many amps can be delivered in 30 seconds at 60 degrees Fahrenheit (or for some, 32 degrees).

Manufacturers of marine batteries must feel that fishermen are unwilling to fish during a freeze.

Reserve Capacity comes a bit closer to being a useful figure for RVing. This is determined by having the battery deliver 25 amps continuously. The reserve capacity is a figure of how many minutes the battery will be able to produce that current until it is effectively "discharged" to 10.5 volts.

If you multiply the reserve capacity rating by a factor of .65, you can obtain a rough estimate of the number of amp-hours capacity of the battery. Since most RVers won't need a battery to produce that much current for a long period of time, the actual amp-hour capacity of that battery may even be safely assumed to be somewhat higher. That's because the more slowly you discharge a battery, the more useful power it will be able to provide.

Amp-Hour Capacity--the most useful standard for RVers when judging a house battery. Some battery makers call it the "20 hour rating." Here the rating is simple: How many amps can be taken from a battery before it is discharged to 10.5 volts over 20 hours of continuous use.

Putting it All Together

If you're still with us, we'll put all this information together in a practical way. On page 11 you'll find a "Sample Power Consumption Worksheet," that shows one RVer's daily power needs of 44 amps (we rounded down to make it easier).

Remember the rule of thumb on battery selection: Always figure what you need then *double it* to avoid discharging a battery to less than half its capacity. So in our example, our boondocker should have at least 88 amp-hours of available battery capacity. MORE IS BETTER! "Save it for a rainy day" applies to cloudy days when solar panels are producing little, or windless days when your wind turbine stands as still as a rabbit when the fox is near.

When shopping then, our RVer should look for a battery with at least 88 amp-hour capacity. If he can't find a deep cycle battery rated in amp-hours, then the reserve capacity rating will need to be at least 135 minutes. (135 x .65 = 87.75).

But what if you can't find a battery with a big enough amp-hour or reserve capacity rating? Or what if your own daily power consumption is higher than what one battery can provide? Then you'll need to purchase more than one deep cycle battery and connect these batteries together properly to provide the needed capacity--we'll come to wiring issues a little later.

One more note on battery capacity: If you'll be using a power inverter, you'll need to concern yourself with its effect on battery banks. Take a minute to check out page 57.

Types of Deep Cycle Batteries

You're still not quite out of the woods. As you peruse the battery shelves at your RV parts store you'll not only find a variety of battery makers, but likely more than one type of deep cycle battery. They are the common lead acid (or flooded acid) battery, and the more expensive gell-cell battery. Even more recently a new upstart has hit the battery neighborhood, touting a technology its maker calls "Spiralcell."

What are the differences? Conventional flooded acid batteries are relatively inexpensive and dependable. For their size, flooded acid batteries provide the greatest amount of amp-hour capacity of all the deep cycles. That's an important consideration if you have limited battery storage space.

On the other hand, lead-acid batteries require regular maintenance. This means popping the lids open and checking out the electrolyte levels. If they're low--below the split ring--they need to be filled up to the ring with distilled water. These conventional cells also give off hydrogen gas when charged. Can you say, "Hindenburg" or "Explosion"? That means you can't just drop a flooded acid battery in any old compartment--the compartment needs to breath--and be away from any source of sparks or flame.

Lead acid batteries have a nasty way of taking a premature death if stored away on a less-than-full charge. And spilled electrolyte will raise all kinds of havoc.

Gell cell batteries are completely sealed and can't be opened. Because their electrolyte is gelled, rather than in a liquid form, a tipped over gell battery won't leak dangerous contents. Hydrogen gas given off by gell cell under charge automatically recombines with oxygen. The result here is that under normal use, a gell battery doesn't need to be "topped off" as there is no electrolyte depletion. And happily, under normal circumstances, a gell battery doesn't give off explosive hydrogen gas[2]. Gell cell batteries tend to charge more quickly than their flooded acid cousins. For boondockers, this can be a real blessing.

Other positive attributes that "gells" can claim include a longer life, as they generally have a higher discharge/recharge

---

[2] Overcharged gell batteries will give off hydrogen gas, and it is usually released through a special vent. This will damage the battery, and can create an explosion hazard.

cycle life. Left in a partially charged state, they won't deteriorate like a flooded acid battery.

With all this good, why not just go with gell batteries? All that convenience comes with a price--at the cash register. Amp-hour for amp-hour, gell batteries cost more. And as we mentioned in the footnote, gell batteries can be damaged by improper charging. We'll come back to that shortly.

Now for that third type of deep cycle battery: Spiralcell technology, marketed in batteries bearing the brand name, "Optima." The company tried out this technology for several years in SLI (starting) batteries, and eventually brought the technology to deep cycles.

The electrolyte in an Optima battery is closer to a gell than a flooded-acid battery, and the company says the construction of the battery allows it to accept a faster rate of charge than most deep cycles. They also claim their design eliminates the dangers associated with improper battery charging.

Like gell cells, Optima says their battery produces a high number of discharge/recharge cycles, and that it can also be used as an SLI battery. This could be the ideal choice for those rare motorhomes where the starting battery doubles as the house battery. Finally, Optima says their batteries are virtually impervious to vibration damage.

But like your Aunty always told you, there's no such thing as a free lunch. Optima deep cycle batteries are expensive--more than typical flooded-acid and gell cells. Optima batteries aren't real high in terms of amp-hour capacity either. You'd need several for any serious boondocking activity.

The Golf Cart "Solution"

Golf cart batteries deserve special attention. These fellows are conventional flooded acid cell batteries with little bit of a twist: The plates in golf cart batteries are much thicker than conventional RV or marine deep cycle batteries. This gives them an advantage in that they have an increased number of expected discharge and recharge cycles.

Since they're designed to push around heavy golf carts (and heavy golfers), they're likewise heavy on amp-hour capacity. But since they're six volt batteries, and most RVers need 12 volts (or 24 for "bus nuts"), you'll need a *minimum* of two of these critters to get your 12 volt requirement. Still, dollar for dollar, many boondockers swear by golf cart batteries.

Not long ago another entrant hit the six volt RV battery field. Marketed by the Rolls Battery Company, Rolls batteries have the same "footprint" as a typical golf cart battery but they stand a bit taller. They also have a great deal more amp-hour capacity. Two of the Rolls' "entry level" RV batteries will store more power than four golf cart batteries but use only half the floor space. The company also claims a huge longevity, suggesting as many as seven years of life in typical RV use. That's considerably more than a golf cart battery. But again, you get what you pay for. Rolls batteries are far more expensive than golf cart batteries.

While we'll come to "hooking up" information on batteries, you should know this: When connecting multiple 12 volt batteries, you'll be wiring in "parallel." The amp-hour capacity of paralleled batteries is the sum of the amp hours of the batteries.

However, when connecting multiple six volt batteries for a 12 volt system, you'll need to "series" wire them. Here the battery amp-hour capacities should be the same, and they DON'T add up.

This means two 12 volt batteries, each with a capacity of 80 amp-hours, equals a total of 160 amp-hours of capacity. But two golf-cart batteries, each with a capacity of say, 85 amp-hours, wired in series gives only a total amp-hour capacity of 85 amp-hours. Yes, you can combine more golf cart batteries to increase the total of your battery "bank account." For example, two *sets* of golf cart batteries in our example would produce twice the amp hour capacity, or 170 amp-hours.

Battery Buying Decisions

Where does all this leave you as a buyer? Deep in the field of decision. Pocketbooks may dictate your choice in some cases. Limited on battery storage space? You can stick a gell cell battery under the dinette seat without a worry about venting. Or maybe Rolls batteries put in a vented compartment will help when you have limited "footprint" space.

Once you choose the type of battery, shop for the size that most closely fits your needs, using that rule of thumb of twice the amount of storage capacity than your projected daily amp-hour use.

Compare more than price, too. Look closely at warranty promises. While most all RV and marine deep cycle batteries come with a 100% replacement guarantee for a short period of time, it's the "prorate" that can kill you. Typically, the full "warranty life" is broken down into blocks of months. The farther you move away from the purchase date, the less you'll get in terms of replacement dollars. And sad to say, most golf cart battery manufacturers don't offer any replacement warranty.

If your journeys take you far from home, find out where you can get your battery replaced if it dies while away from the original point of purchase.

Hook 'em Up!

First, a word about safety: Take off your jewelry before working on battery systems. A ring or watch "welded" to a battery post can be a major health trauma. Put on eye protection, battery acid will damage your optics.

Putting in a replacement battery is easy: Remove the old battery, clean the connectors, and while observing proper polarity (terminals go back on the same way they came off), hook up the terminals and physically secure the new battery. By secure, check to make sure it won't tip or vibrate. Replace any worn tie downs.

What if your calculations showed you needed more storage capacity than a single battery allows? Or maybe you've decided to switch to six volt batteries to replace a single 12-volter. Then certain battery rules apply:

Parallel Wiring

Batteries of the same voltages must be wired in parallel, that is, positive post to positive post, and negative post to negative post. The "house" wiring running from the RV is then connected to the appropriate terminals of <u>one</u> of the batteries.

As we learned, paralleled batteries **add** amp-hour capacity. You may parallel as many batteries as you like to increase storage capacity. But remember--when paralleling batteries, always start with new batteries with identical specifications-- preferably the same model battery from the same manufacturer.

Why so? Because paralleled batteries will "feed" off one another. If you parallel an older, weaker battery to a new one, the new one will attempt to "feed" its weaker mate, eventually killing both batteries. To see how batteries are wired in parallel, see the diagram on page 32.

Series Wiring

If you're attempting to use six-volt batteries to power a twelve-volt system, you're looking to obtain an increase in voltage. In this case you'll need to series wire batteries together. As you recall, you will add the voltages together (6 volts + 6 volts = 12 volts), but you will NOT increase the storage capacity.

In series wiring the positive post of one battery is wired to the negative post of the other battery. The "house" wiring then connects to the remaining two free posts. Again, we recommend you observe the same rules on pairing up batteries as before--the same battery specifications, preferably the same model and manufacturer. To see how batteries are wired in series, see the diagram on page 33.

Series-Parallel Wiring

To increase the amp-hour capacity of your lower voltage batteries, you may parallel battery "banks" together, for example, if you have two pairs of six volt golf cart batteries. Each "set" of these batteries is series wired, positive post of one to the negative post of its mate. THEN wire the free positive posts of each of the pairs to each other; the free negative posts of the pairs are then wired together. The house wiring attaches to the "paired" posts that connect the sets together. Finally, to see how batteries are wired in series-parallel, see the diagram on page 34.

Keep Your Batteries Alive

After putting all that money and effort into the purchase and installation of your batteries, you'll want to keep that investment as long as you can. Batteries are like expensive pets: They require some attention--but thankfully, no scooper.

It's best to set a regular maintenance schedule for your batteries. If your batteries are the flooded-acid type, they'll need to have their electrolyte levels checked and topped off. If you've invested in gell cell technology, you won't be having to look after your batteries as often as flooded cell owners, but both types need to have their terminals checked for security. As you bounce down the road, your rig takes a lot of jarring and vibration. Loose connections on batteries spell trouble.

To cut down on maintenance time, some boondockers invest in special battery caps that reduce the amount of electrolyte loss. Inside the caps are chemicals that act to recover the hydrogen gas given off during the charge cycle. This catalyst recombines the hydrogen gas with oxygen to form water, which then drips back into the cells. Marketed under a variety of trade names such as "HydroCaps," these vent caps do have some merit. In our experience, however, they don't completely eliminate the need to occasionally "top off" the cells with distilled water[3]. Yuck it up, gell cell owners--you don't need battery caps!

---

[3] Tap water may contain minerals or other chemicals that can decrease the life of your battery.

Just how often you'll need to check your electrolyte levels will vary. How you recharge your batteries can affect the gassing rate--and hence how fast the electrolyte level drops. Until you get a "handle" on how often you need to top off the cells, it's wise to check them frequently--a couple of times a month.

Even then, your batteries should not "drink" excessive amounts of water. One rule of thumb says that a battery cell should take no more than two ounces of water for every 30 to 50 hours of charging. If more consumption is shown, then you're likely overcharging your batteries, which will lead to premature failure.

Keep the tops of your batteries clean. Dirt across the tops can actually allow a small flow of current to cross over, discharging the batteries. If the battery terminals show corrosion, then make up a paste of baking soda and water and carefully clean up the corrosion. DON'T allow this mixture to get into the cells!

Some battery users coat their battery terminals with petroleum jelly. We find that a bit messy, so we use battery terminal "patches" sold in auto parts stores. These reduce the corrosion problem without making a gooey mess.

It's worth repeating: Always ensure that you have plenty of ventilation to the battery compartment when charging flooded-acid type batteries. And don't store any sensitive electrical equipment in a battery compartment.

Battery State of Charge

One limitation on battery life is the number of times it can be discharged and recharged. Even though deep cycle batteries are designed for repeated charging cycles, they will last longer if not too deeply discharged. To that end, it's best to not allow a battery to become more than 50% discharged.

How do you know how "low" your batteries are? Don't rely on the stock "battery level meters" typically included with your factory instrument package. "Good, Fair, Bad" indicators aren't specific enough to really know what's going on "under the hood." Invest in a digital multimeter.

This piece of electronic test equipment will prove invaluable for tracking down electrical problems, or even just keeping an eye on your batteries. You can buy one for around $20 or more, but regardless of how much you spend, *read the instruction book before you use it!*

To check your battery state of charge, set your meter to the appropriate setting for DC voltage in the range you'd anticipate your battery to read. Connect the meter probes to the terminals where your house wiring connects to the battery bank. Be sure to observe polarity! Some meters are forgiving, and will allow a reversed polarity--others show their temper by dying.

The reading you take from this hookup will show you the voltage level for the entire battery bank. Using the chart, "Battery State of Charge," you'll know how close you are to being "out of gas." While the chart was based on a 77 degree temperature, recognize that the colder things get, the less efficient the battery is.

BATTERY STATE OF CHARGE

Battery Voltage	Remaining Capacity
12.63	100 %
12.54	90%
12.45	80%
12.36	70%
12.27	60%
12.18	50%
12.09	40%
12	30%
11.91	20%
11.82	10%

(Based on 77 degree f. ambient temperature)

Parallel wiring increases storage capacity

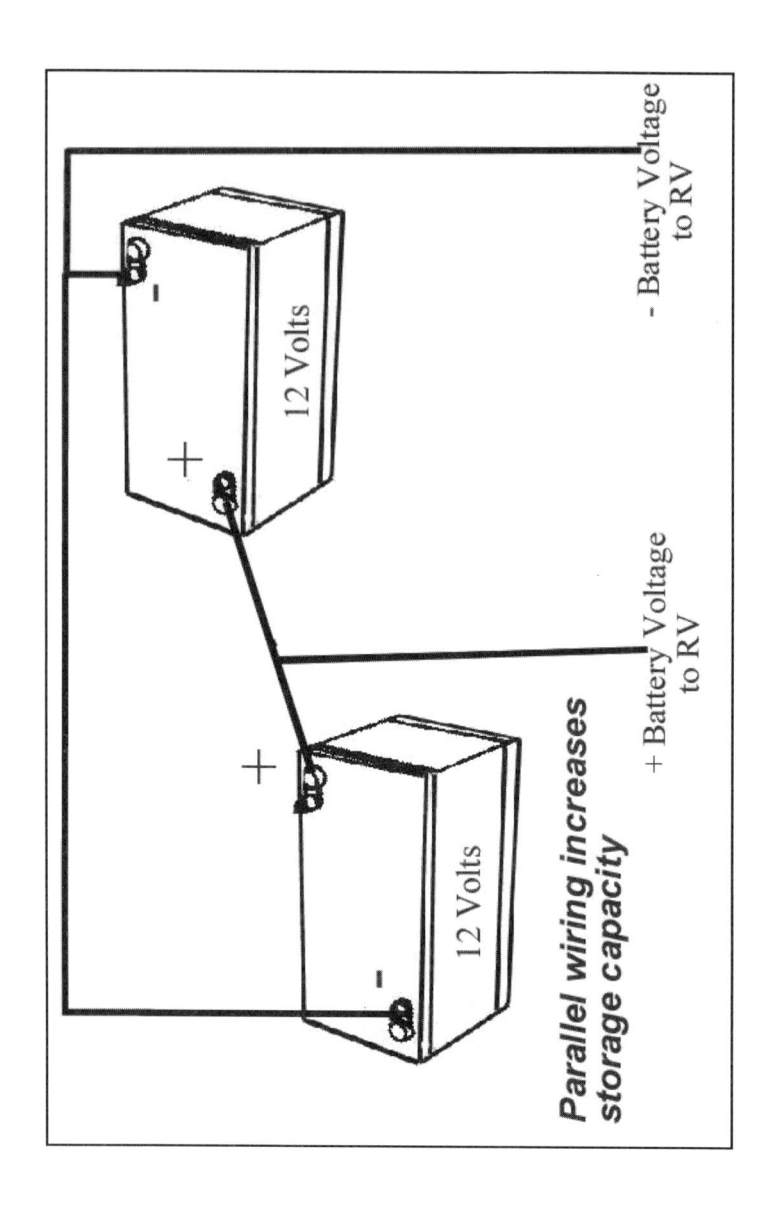

Series wiring increases voltage output

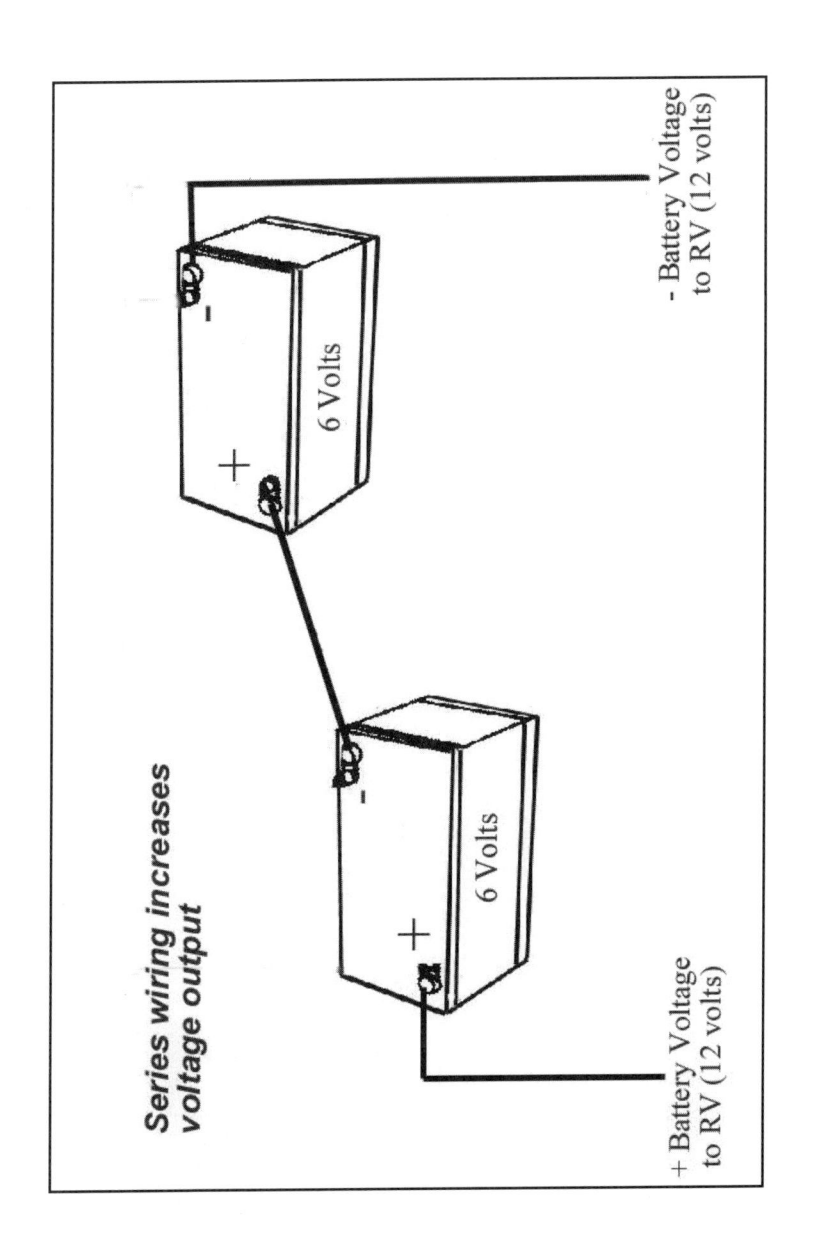

6 Volts

6 Volts

− Battery Voltage to RV (12 volts)

+ Battery Voltage to RV (12 volts)

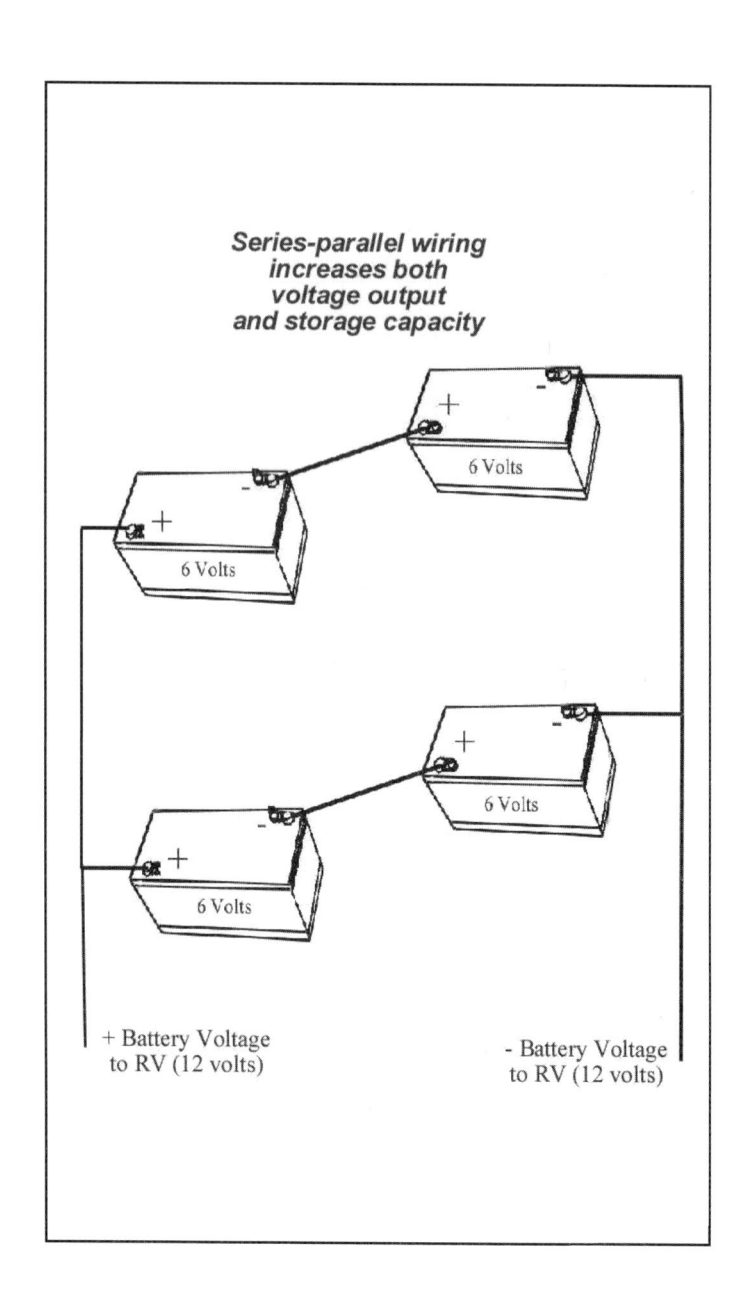

***Series-parallel wiring
increases both
voltage output
and storage capacity***

6 Volts

6 Volts

6 Volts

6 Volts

+ Battery Voltage
to RV (12 volts)

− Battery Voltage
to RV (12 volts)

CHAPTER 3
Solar: Let Sol Make Your Power

Ah, solar power. Quiet and efficient, and low maintenance by nature. The only regular attention solar panels require is an occasional cleaning to remove dust. Most boondockers place their solar panels on the roof. Once in place, panels are out of the way in an otherwise unused piece of real-estate.

Solar panels will easily outlive your rig; their warranty periods often running 20 years or longer. In reality, solar panels often last longer than their warranty. With a cost of about $4.00 per watt, the initial outlay is more than the cost of a fossil-fueled generator, but amortized over the life period (and with the benefit of no further fuel or expensive maintenance) their cost is rather attractive.

Types of Solar Panels

In the RV world there are basically two types of solar panel: Crystalline or film. The latter is extremely strong--salesmen sometimes jump up and down on them to demonstrate their strength. They cost a bit more than their crystalline cousins, but if you mount your panels on the roof and don't transport gorillas in your storage pods, you'll likely find crystalline panels are just fine.

Still, some RVers find film panels (which are somewhat reminiscent of a bathtub mat) are more flexible in use. Flexible indeed! You can bend these panels around corners, hang them from the side of your rig, or put them in places you wouldn't otherwise dream.

Sizing Your System

Earlier we provided worksheets to help you determine your electrical power needs. That power need was tied to battery capacity. When deciding how much solar panel power output you need, it's most easily tied to your battery bank size. A simple rule is this: For each amp-hour of battery capacity, provide 1 watt of solar panel output. Of course, you can reverse this too, ensuring that you have enough battery capacity for the solar panel output you plan. In practice then, a 50 watt solar panel would like to "see" a 100 amp-hour battery bank.

All this assumes good solar output. Panels need exposure to full sunlight to give their rated output--even a small shadow can dramatically reduce power production. And unless you put in a fancy "solar tracking" system, a panel can reasonably expect to receive full sun about six hours per day, maximum. Hence, a 50 watt solar panel on a good, non-cloudy day, can be expected to put out about 300 watts. (50 watts x 6 hours = 300 watts).

So how do you figure out how much solar power you need? Back in Chapter 1 we used a worksheet to figure out your daily power consumption. From there, we learned that the battery bank rule of thumb is twice the amount of amp-hour capacity as one day's worth of projected power consumption.

Now apply the solar panel rule of thumb, *in reverse*. For every 100 amp-hours of battery capacity, figure you'll need 50 watts of solar panel. Still, this assumes good solar exposure. If you camp in cloudy areas, you'd be better to figure 75 watts of solar panel output for every 100 amp-hours of battery capacity.

What if you can't afford to install as many solar panels as you would need to match your battery bank? The beauty of solar panels is they can be added--not having to be purchased and installed all at once. Of course, you'll either have to reduce your power consumption to match your solar output, or find another way to recharge your battery bank.

Tilting Panels

If you boondock in winter, consider tilting your panels. Panels are most efficient when the sun falls on them at a 90 degree angle. Since the sun's relative position in the sky drops south with winter, getting full use of solar power requires compensating the angle of the panel.

The chart on the next page helps to decipher how to set your panel angle. The chart lists major cities on opposite sides of the continent, and gives *approximate* latitudes for them. Find your location along a parallel between these major cities, then use the associated information to determine your angle of tilt.

For example, if you're staked out in Quartzsite, Arizona, you're on approximately the same parallel as Los Angeles and Wilmington--about 34 degrees. You'll want to tilt your solar panels to about 43 degrees, as measured from the flat surface of your roof.

Cities	Approx. Latitude	Tilt Panel Angle
Brownsville, TX; Key West, FL	25	25
Corpus Christi, TX; Tampa, FL	28	31
Austin, TX; Saint Augstine, FL	30	35
Tucson, AZ; Savannah, GA	32	39
Los Angeles, CA; Wilmington, SC	34	43
Las Vegas, NV; Raleigh, NC	36	47
San Francisco, CA; Richmond, VA	38	51
Redding, CA; Philadelphia, PA	40	55
Medford, OR; Providence, RI	42	49
Eugene, OR; Portland, ME	44	63
Portland, OR; Duluth, MN	46	66
Everett, WA; Grand Forks, MN	48	68

Chart 3-1 **Solar Panel Tilt**

All this requires orienting the position of your RV, relative to the sun's path, appropriate to your solar panels. If you find yourself in a position where you can't park your RV to take advantage of tilting your panels, you'll be stuck with your panels laying flat. In a case like that, consider adding more solar panels to increase your net solar power output.

Temperature can also effect the efficiency of solar power. As temperature increases, efficiency decreases. Despite high solar output, a summer day may actually decrease solar power output. How panels are affected varies. Nevertheless, on a hot summer day, rooftop temperatures will cut power output.

Solar Panel Tilt System

If you solar panels aren't already equipped with a tilt system, here's one "after market" suggested system.

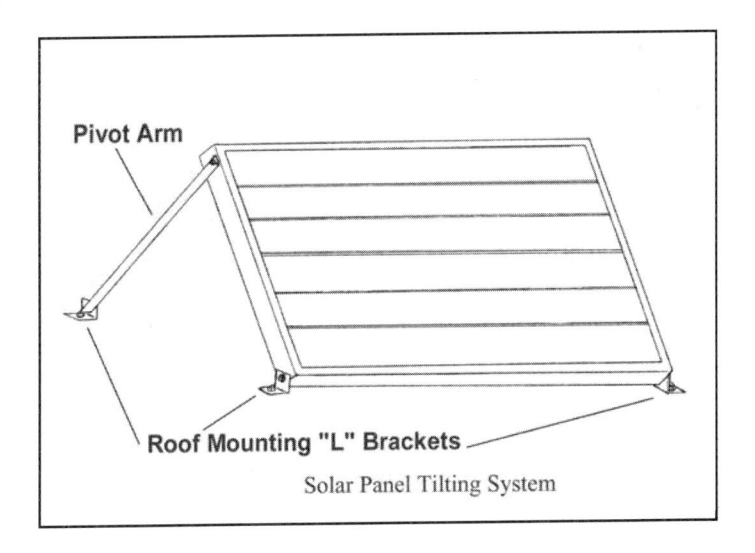

Solar Panel Tilting System

The basis of the system is the use of roof mounted "L" brackets. These should be attached to sturdy roof members, be it a plywood deck, or cross members. Placement of the brackets is near the panel corners. If you cannot find solid surfaces to screw into, your alternative is to purchase and install "Well Nuts." You can find these at specialty hardware supply stores. Well nuts are a rubber expansion plug system. An appropriate size hole is drilled through the roof material, the well nut inserted, and then the expansion plug is mushroomed open with a bolt.

Lay the solar panel flat on the roof to act as a template. Place the four L brackets near the corners of the panel, allowing a small amount of distance between the brackets and the panel edges--say about 1/8". Mark the location of the brackets, and remove the solar panel. Now mount the L brackets to the roof, using screws or well nuts, as described above. With the four L brackets securely mounted, return the solar panel to position, and place shims under the panel to raise it to a level where a 1/4" hole can be safely drilled through the edge of the L bracket, on into the side of the panel frame. Be careful! Don't drill into the solar panel backing--you may ruin the panel!

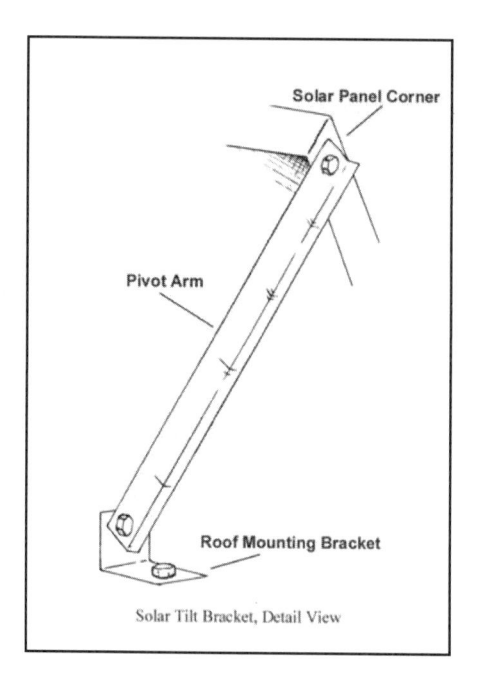

Solar Tilt Bracket, Detail View

Now determine which edge of the panel will be the "bottom" when the panel is tilted. Run a 1/4" bolt through from the outside edge of the L bracket, through to the inside of the panel frame. Equip the bolt with washer and locknut. This will form the pivot point of the panel. Repeat for the opposite corner of the "lower" end of the solar panel.

Next, fashion and install the pivot arm. The material here is a piece of 1/4" angle steel (or aluminum). A 1/4" hole is drilled through the end of the angle steel, and this is bolted to one of the free roof mounted L brackets. Determine the appropriate location for the next hole by tilting the panel to the appropriate angle for catching the winter sun. Place the free end of the angle steel next to the solar panel frame "upper" hole and mark the steel. Some folks locate several hole "locations" to allow them to adjust their panel tilt for multiple locations.

With drill location(s) marked on the steel, drill 1/4" holes. Raise the panel to meet the pivot arm hole, and install bolt, washer, and locknut. Repeat for the second pivot arm.

Yes, you can orient your panels in either a vertical or horizontal fashion. Horizontal mounting may reduce the risk of wind damage; vertical orientation is good where roof "real estate" is at a premium.

In practice, lower the panels and mount all four corners to the roof L brackets when traveling. If high winds threaten, it's best to lower and lock down the panels in the same way.

Solar Panel Regulation

To safely and effectively use solar panels, some form of charge regulation is required. There are *self-regulated* panels available, but the power output of these panels makes them impractical for anything other than simply maintaining a fully charged battery.

Solar panel regulators do more than just prevent battery overcharging, they also protect the batteries against discharging at night. A solar panel directly attached to a battery bank will deplete it. As soon as the voltage produced by the panel is less than that of the battery, the flow of current will march right out of the battery and into the solar panel. Special electrical components known as *diodes* act like "one way electrical valves," that allow electricity to flow only from the panel to the battery, not in reverse. Panel regulators have diodes built in to prevent discharge. Most also provide fuses for protection against overloads.

Commercially produced solar panel regulators are like a visit to a coffee shop. You can get just plain old regulators to fancy regulators "with all the bells and whistles." The latter may have built-in meters that show battery voltage and solar panel output. We've found that the latter type can be quite helpful, but aren't absolutely necessary. You can use your digital multimeter to verify battery voltage. By keeping track of your consumption, and comparing it to your state of charge, you'll know in short order if your panels aren't "putting out."

Whatever regulator you invest in, try and get one that is rated to handle more current than your initial solar panel installation produces. This allows you to expand your solar panel "farm," if your needs increase without having to go out and buy a larger regulator.

Solar Installation

While the details of solar panel installation are beyond the scope of this book, it can be said that many RVers can--and do--install their own solar systems. Bear in mind you will have to drill holes in your roof to secure the solar panels. Generally, wiring can be run down the refrigerator roof vent, or alternatively, down a plumbing vent.

When installing panels, keep in mind that shadows falling on panels reduce their output--dramatically. Placing them away from obvious shade makers like the TV antenna or air conditioner unit is wise. Solar panels need solid support anywhere they attach to the roof. This could mean attaching them to roof rafters, if spaced properly. If you have a solid plywood roof deck under your roofing, then placement isn't much of a problem. If not, and rafter spacing is inadequate, you might consider installing a metal frame over the rafters, then attaching the solar panels to the frame.

Since crystalline panels are subject to damage, be cautious when taking your rig under low hanging branches. A good heavy poke with a tree limb can break a solar panel, proving a most costly mistake.

Solar Maintenance

Solar panels require little maintenance. Ensuring the panels are kept clean and free of debris (think leaves) is the largest maintenance investment. Most panels can be cleaned with a damp rag. If you spend much time in a rainy environment, you could actually develop a scummy coating on your panels. In that case, follow the panel maker's instructions as to what cleaning solution to use. We use spray-on window glass cleaner and a soft rag when ours get out of hand.

CHAPTER 4
Turbines--The Answer's Blowin' in the Wind

Put aside visions of water pumping "wind mills" of the Old West. Modern, power-generating wind turbines are compact, light, and highly efficient.

Wind turbines are practical where there's a constant source of wind. Folks who boondock along the coasts, the plains states, in the Rockies, and in some areas of the desert Southwest are generally candidates for wind power. Keep in mind though, that many factors influence wind flow: Weather patterns and terrain can create interesting results. Identical wind turbines placed even a few feet apart may produce different power outputs at the same time, a result of how winds are affected by terrain, buildings, etc.

Like solar panels, wind turbines are weather dependent. When clouds block the sun, solar has its problems. Let the winds drop and your turbine blades stand motionless--no juice, pardner. But as part of an overall alternative power system, wind is hard to beat. Combine wind with solar, and you have amazing potential.

Wind driven power systems are some of the least expensive of the array of RV energy options. A popular wind turbine among RVers runs in the mid $400 range, and produces 400 watts of power in a 28 mile per hour wind. You could easily spend nearly $1500 for solar panels to produce an equivalent amount of power.

For us, a combination of solar and wind power works well. With winters on the Sonora Desert, the sun shines a lot. Even when the clouds roll in, the desert winds provide a fairly constant blow from January clear until the time to us to move along in April. Up in the Pacific Northwest, we spend a bit of time doing coastal camping. As you know, there are two seasons in the Northwest--the cold rainy season and the warm rainy season. Solar may be out the question, but the wind is free.

A Wind Power Disadvantage?

On the surface, using a wind turbine for boondockers sounds almost like a dream come true: Small equipment investment, little maintenance, free "power supply." There is a dark side to the wind turbine world: Noise.

While a solar panel just lies around on the RV roof producing power silently, a wind turbine is a mechanical device. In operation, it does make some amount of noise. How much noise?

To produce usable power, smaller wind turbines spin at a much faster rate than larger ones. The faster the spin rate, the greater the potential for noise. To add to the issue, when a wind turbine comes close to its maximum power output, that noise may become intense (see *"Governing or Regulation System"* below).

Will this noise be more than you can tolerate? That's a personal question. The best way to check this is to visit wind turbine owners when their machines are operating. Listen closely, particularly when the winds are high, and see for yourself if the noise is acceptable or not.

Sizing and Selection

Sizing the wind system is a bit trickier than calculating solar panel needs. The wind is not a constant; however wind maps do help to gauge an average over time. Since wind power, like solar, can be "added on," perhaps the best way to approach the matter is to start with one wind turbine and upgrade if and when you determine you need more muscle.

While there are several wind turbine manufacturers, few wind turbines are RV-friendly. This is largely due to physical weight and size of turbines. The larger the output, the heavier the turbine weight and the size of the blades. Since RVers generally look for systems that are easy to handle and offer fast set-up and take down, going to a system that offers much more than a few hundred watts of power can seriously stretch the typical RVers abilities and time constraints.

Wind turbine comparisons are made in several areas. Of primary interest is power output. Unlike solar panels, making comparisons of power output between wind turbines is not always easy. Here are a few things to look at:

Rated Output: Rated output is the manufacturer's statement of power output, at a given (manufacturer choosen) speed. The problem is not everyone uses the same wind speed to list their rated output. However, a little bit of the relationship of wind speed to power-output can help you make comparisons.

Wind speed relative to power is not on a linear scale. That is to say, if a given wind turbine produces 150 watts at 15 miles per hour, it produces far more than 300 watts (double the power) at 30 miles per hour (double the speed). Rather, the relationship is this: Double the wind speed, multiply the output power by a factor of eight. Hence, in our example, our 150 watts at 15 miles per hour should (in theory) produce 1200 watts at 30 miles per hour.

We say "in theory," because blade efficiency and other factors may not make the calculations "perfect." Still, for purposes of comparison, it will help to make side by side comparisons. Working the equation backwards can help.

Let's say you're comparing two wind turbines, "Brand A" provides its rating at 28 miles per hour, where "Brand B" at 14 miles per hour. Brand A produces 800 watts at 28 miles per hour, while Brand B produces 400 watts at 14 miles per hour. Which produces more power?

Brand A, running at 14 miles per hour, is running at half its rated wind speed. Our power-to-wind speed relationship tells us that half the power means an eighth of the power. 1/8 of 800 watts is only 100 watts, while Brand B, running along at that speed is producing 400 watts--a major difference for my money.

Peak Output: This is the manufacturer's rating of the maximum power produced by their system just prior to its entering "governing," or "regulation." These two terms refer to a wind turbine's way of protecting itself from high winds. Without some method of governing or regulation, a wind turbine could burn itself out from over power, or could physically tear itself up.

Cut-in Speed: This is the wind speed required before the turbine begins to produce electrical power. Folks laugh when they drive by our winter boondock spot. Why? Our next door neighbor (and good friend) has a wind turbine, made by different firm than ours. His turbine will be spinning away, while ours looks like a dead duck--no motion. Invariably we get a lot of ribbing about how "powerful" our wind turbine is.

But all it takes is a quick check of power output to settle the issue. Even while our friend's turbine is spinning, it isn't necessarily producing power--simply putting on a show. Since a lot of the ribbing we take comes from him, we just feed it back, letting him know that he'll probably be replacing his rotor bearings a lot more often than we will, for the same amount of "real" power generated!

Swept Area: In reality, when comparing wind turbines of various kinds, one of the least spoken of terms may actually be the most useful. Swept area is the measure of just how much area of the wind the machine can "catch." The larger the swept area, the greater the potential electrical power output. Since most turbines operate at around the same efficiency, as a rule of thumb a turbine with a larger swept area will produce more power.

Voltage Output: Be careful here. Not all wind turbines will produce power in a form you can use. The voltage output of the machine must be compatible with your battery storage system. Hence, the typical RVer will need a wind turbine that produces 12-volt DC power. Some turbines can be "tapped" to produce a variety of voltages, including bus-popular 24 volts.

Blade Material: Blades are the heart of the wind generating system. Most wind turbines useful to RVers have blades made of a composite material, often plastic with embedded carbon fibers.

Maximum Design Wind Speed: Will high winds demolish your wind turbine? To look at the estimates of some turbine engineers, a hurricane could pass and leave their systems intact. Don't bet the farm on these "estimates," as it's pretty difficult to field test wind turbines with any sort of regularity. Most hurricanes just aren't cooperative enough.

The turbine may weather high winds, but can be torn loose from their mounting systems if rapidly pitched back and forth by wind turbulence. This is a special problem for RVers. Why? Because RVers don't usually mount their turbines on high towers. The closer to the ground, the higher the wind turbulence. We've been pulled out of bed at 3:00 in the morning when an unexpected storm has passed through, and our turbine has cast about like a dog having fits. Fortunately, our tower system has allowed us to safely lower our turbine and lash it despite howling gales.

Shut Down Mechanism: There are times when you may not want your turbine to operate. Perhaps it's time for maintenance, or a high wind may cause you some heart palpitations. How do you shut the thing down? There are two different systems used on commercial wind turbines. Mechanical systems allow the operator to turn or furl the turbine tail, taking the machine's nose out of the wind, effectively stalling it. The other method is electrical, called "dynamic braking."

A dynamic braking system simply uses a switch to electrically short circuit the turbine's alternator, causing enough resistance to stall out the rotor system. Of the wind turbine systems used by RVers, we've only encountered dynamic braking systems, never mechanical. On our turbine the dynamic brake works great, every time. However, our neighbor's system does have a bit of a flaw: Sometimes his dynamic brake works, and sometimes it doesn't. Experience shows that our friend's system invariably has problems when winds are high--not a good time to find you can't shut the system down! At times he's found that waiting for the wind to slow slightly, then kicking the switch again will have the desired result.

Governing or Regulation System: As mentioned, each manufacturer has its way of keeping their turbine system under control in high winds. Each should have a way of shutting itself down at a given maximum speed. Among RV-popular wind turbines, there are two governing systems. The first ("Whisper") tilts the rotor up and out of the wind. The other ("AIR") finds its answer in blade design. In this case when the winds reach the maximum rated speed, the blades actually twist (elastically), reducing the amount of wind that can be converted into power.

It should be noted that some folks find this blade-twisting design makes an objectionably loud noise. To counter the problem, the latest generation of AIR machines uses an automatic dynamic braking system to shut itself down prior to hitting the "noise point." Some users don't like losing the extra wattage that lies between the dynamic break cutoff and that which the blades themselves provide.

Once top governing speed is reached, you can expect a sudden drop-off in power--often to almost no charging power.

Tower Top Weight: Finally, the last measurement is the weight of that which mounts on the turbine tower. This includes the weight of the turbine itself, including all its parts (tail, rotor, yaw, etcetera).

Towers

A chief concern of a wind turbine owner is a strong, secure wind turbine mounting system. Turbine blades can 'spin up' to amazing speeds; a finger, hand, even an arm, can be severed if caught by a spinning turbine blade assembly. Wind turbines must be mounted high enough that they don't endanger passerby.

Notwithstanding, the higher above the ground, the better the results, as winds are actually reduced by friction as they 'scrub' across the ground. Objects on the ground also reduce the relative wind speed. Think of it like a twig floating down a stream. In the middle of the stream is a large rock, wide and tall. As the twig approaches the rock you'll notice that its speed drops dramatically. The cause? Turbulence created by the rush of water meeting the resistance of the rock. For us, keeping the turbine as high above the ground as practical will give us more effective wind power.

Mounting a wind turbine on a "tower" system is a critical matter. ALWAYS follow the manufacturer's recommendations as to minimum sizing of tower materials. This need not be as complicated as you might imagine.

For example, we use an AIR 403 wind turbine, manufactured by Southwest Windpower. The tower top weight is only about 14 pounds, and the recommended mount is 1 1/4" thick wall steel electrical conduit. We initially mounted ours on a truck camper, six feet above the roof on a conduit mast. When we were moving down the highway, we'd take the rotor assembly off and lay the turbine down on the roof, securing it against movement.

Later we moved into a fifth wheel trailer. In this instance, we built a "telescoping" mast system. The top 10 foot section was 1 1/4" electrical conduit, which during travel mode, slide down into a length of 1 1/2" conduit. The larger tube was stepped onto the trailer's rear bumper, and a heavy bracket locked onto the top of this larger tube, close to roof level.

On location we would release the mast from the upper bracket and lower it and the turbine to the ground, as the "step" was hinged. We'd then pull the upper mast section up, "telescoping" it out of the lower section. A heavy pin held the upper section from collapsing into the lower. With the rotor assembly installed, we'd then lift the whole works back upright and secure it in the upper bracket.

All of this met manufacturer's specifications, and although it was a bit unwieldy, the system worked. We could have the turbine up and operating in about 15 minutes.

Today we have a system we feel is far superior. Constructed of tubular aluminum, it likewise telescopes into itself, but is equipped with a crank system that allows us to simply turn a handle to raise and lower the turbine. Quick, easy, and secure. Unfortunately, the system is a prototype from a company that has since folded. It's a great innovation, and perhaps someone else will pick up on the idea and make it available to RVers.

Some RVers have found that a roof access ladder makes a good place to mount a turbine mast. If you choose such a plan, be sure the ladder is SECURELY mounted into framing members of the RV.

Mounting your turbine on your RV is not a requirement. We've seen plenty of other RVers who have mounted their turbines beside their rigs, perhaps using the rig as one part of the assembly, and using earth as the physical mast step. Others have set up their masts away from their rigs. In such cases, guy wires often become necessary for additional support.

In any event, *always* follow the minimum standards provided by your turbine manufacturer. Having a wind turbine "fail" and come down on your rig could cause serious damage--if not physical injury. And remember too, the motorhomer in Yuma who forgot to lower his wind turbine before heading out on the freeway. Everything went fine--until he went under a freeway overpass. We're told the entire rear wall of his coach was sheared off the back of the rig when the turbine caught the overpass. That's enough to ruin your *whole* day.

Installation

Once the matter of turbine installation is conquered, the rest is, "downhill all the way." Most of the turbine systems used by RVers have internal voltage regulators, and wiring is fairly straight forward.

Typically three wires run down the inside of the mast, a positive, negative, and ground wire lead. These MUST be sized appropriately, as a wind turbine can produce a large amount of power. If wiring is too small, not only can efficiency losses make your system nearly useless, they can also run dangerously hot. Always follow the turbine manufacturer's recommendations for wire size.

It is best to run your turbine wiring directly to the battery bank, via a circuit breaker. Yes, you may be able to use the RV frame as one "leg" of the power circuit. If your manufacturer suggests the use of a ground rod, USE IT. While it may not spare you damage from a direct lightening strike, it could save you a lot of grief from static electricity charge buildup.

As mentioned, our turbine uses "dynamic braking" to shut it down. Originally we used an electrical switch obtained from an auto parts supply house. It was a common, heavy amperage toggle switch, meeting recommendations, but it lasted only a couple of years. We later shopped around and purchased an ancient knife switch and installed it in a weatherproof box at the base of the turbine mast. It looks "Frankenstien-esque," but we've never had another switch problem.

Operation and Maintenance

When we boondock in an area of wind, we simply "run up" the wind turbine, flip the switch on, and sit back and let the system operate.

We do keep a "weather eye peeled" for any upcoming storms. If strong winds are anticipated and we feel at all uncomfortable about them, we simply roll down the turbine and secure the rotor. We know our system, and don't usually get concerned until we hear of winds approaching 60 miles per hour. Of course, at 40 miles per hour our system goes into regulation, as our blades twist. This makes a pretty loud racket, so if our batteries are charged, we simply kick in the dynamic break, and the rotor simply "luffs" along, making virtually no noise.

We are very cautious about ensuring that all mounting hardware is securely tightened. While our turbine manufacturer recommends an annual inspection cycle, we prefer to make a roof top visit every month or two. We ensure that the bolts that hold the blades to the rotor hub are tight, and that the rotor is securely tightened onto the turbine shaft. Mast hardware is critical, particularly where the mast system secures to the roof. We sleep a lot more soundly on a windy night by making frequent checks.

Chapter 5
Inverters: Shore Power--To Go!

Between solar panels, wind power, and a good battery bank, many RVers have plenty of energy--albeit in a "low voltage" package. But 12 volt DC power doesn't do much for running a microwave oven or other shore power hungry devices. Boondockers like having conveniences, too. A power inverter makes it possible.

For our purposes, a power inverter changes 12 volt (or 24 volt) DC power to 120 volt AC power, usable for many appliances and other shore power devices. Can you use an inverter?

Inverter Selection

There are a couple of power inverter "flavors," to consider. The most common among RVers are *modified sine wave* inverters. The power output of these doesn't "look" exactly like shore power, but for most devices it's perfectly acceptable.

More costly *true sine wave* inverters produce nearly power identical to that coming from the local power utility. What might you need a true sine wave inverter for? Many laser printers find modified sine wave power disagreeable; *some* battery recharging systems also need true sine wave power. If you have any question as to whether what you want to power with an inverter will operate on a modified sine wave, contact that device's manufacturer.

Sizing your inverter is important: Too small, and you won't be able to power some equipment. Too large? Then you may squeeze your pocketbook, as the larger the inverter, the greater the cost. The inverter you choose must be able to produce enough output power to provide for all shore power equipment that you'll run at the same time. In our case, a 1500 watt inverter was large enough for us, since our microwave oven needs 1200 watts to operate. We simply don't operate any other shore power equipment when using the microwave.

Whenever turned on an inverter draws some amount of power, or *standby current*. Ours draws 1 amp every hour in standby. For a boondocker this is a significant load--bordering the sacrilegious--so we always turn our inverter off when not in use. To make this an easier operation, we made sure our inverter was capable of remote control, as our inverter is mounted outside of the coach. Running inside and outside to flip a switch just didn't appeal to us. Remote controls are hardwired to an inside switch.

Some high-end inverters also provide battery charging capability. That is, when plugged into shore power utilities, the inverter will charge the RV house battery bank. These can be fairly sophisticated and produce a high rate of charge, and are often "smart" chargers that are excellent for the needs of RV deep cycle batteries.

Power Consumption and Battery Bank

As we discussed earlier, inverters are NOT super efficient devices; if they were, then for every amp of shore power produced, an inverter would only draw 10 amps of 12 volt battery power. However, reality tells us that the calculation for current draw on batteries is more like this:

Battery amp-hours consumed =

(AC amps x 10) x 1.2 x hours of use

The "1.1" multiplier allows for inverter inefficiency.

Another formula you'll find helpful if you're working with AC watts consumed by the shore power equipment is this:

Battery amp-hours consumed =

(AC watts/12) x 1.2 x hours of use

We earlier touched on this back in Chapter 2 in conjunction with filling out your power consumption worksheets.

All of this is extremely important to your battery bank. A battery bank should never "see" a load greater than one-fourth of its total amp-hour capacity. Stated another way, your battery bank amp-hour capacity should be four times greater than the maximum amp-hour draw placed on it by your inverter. As an example, if your greatest shore power user is a 1200 watt microwave oven, then, 1200 watts/12 x 1.2 = 120 amp-hour draw. A sufficiently sized battery bank would have no less than a 480 amp-hour capacity.

Inverter Installation

An inverter like any sensitive electronic device should not be installed in the same compartment as the battery bank. Battery gassing can damage their circuitry. Keep them out of the same compartment as a gasoline or LP fired generator, as inverters don't do well in an explosive atmosphere.

Still, inverters do chew up a lot of current, so they must be installed as close as possible to the battery bank, as you want to keep cable runs short. Long cable runs or small diameter wiring are often at the root of inverter problems. Follow the inverter maker's instructions as to length of wire runs and always use the minimum gauge wire or larger.

Be sure to observe polarity when wiring up the power leads to the battery bank--reversal almost guarantees an expensive "frying" of inverter circuitry.

Wiring the shore power side of the inverter can be accomplished in one of two ways. Perhaps the most common RV installation is to use the AC "receptacle" provided on most inverters. The RV shore plug is plugged into this receptacle, thus eliminating any danger of plugging into shore power while using inverter power. An alternative is to have a suitable transfer switch installed, as is done for some RV generator installations.

In our installation, we've run a suitably sized electrical cable from the inverter back to our shore power cable compartment. The cable from the inverter is there equipped with a receptacle that fits our shore power plug. When boondocking we leave the shore power plug in that receptacle and only disconnect it on occasions where shore utilities are available.

To prevent our power *converter* (which turns shore power into 12 volt DC power) from drawing power when connected to the inverter, we've equipped the converter with a switch that allows us to isolate it from our rig's shore power circuitry. In a similar vein, some RV refrigerators automatically "roll over" to shore power when they sense its availability. If that's the case for your refrigerator, you'll need to disconnect the shore power cord in the refrigerator rear access compartment whenever using an inverter.

Chapter 6
Fresh Water Wizardry

If you boondock in the same spot for an extended time it's a blessing not to have to lug the rig out for water. Running the rig out twice a week can be wearing.

RVers have come up with some ingenious ways of bringing back plenty of fresh water and getting it into their tanks. We'll touch on the most popular.

Roll Out the Barrel

For those who tow with a pickup, there's usually plenty of room in the truck bed to haul a water barrel or drum. Plastic drums are the most popular as they don't rust, and are lightweight. Make sure whatever drum you use hasn't previously contained items hazardous to your health. "Food grade" drums are the safest bet.

The difficult part of bringing your water home in a barrel is that typically, the sidewalls of the drum are so thick you can't really see the height of the water in the drum. If your RV fresh water tank is smaller than the drum's capacity, you can get stuck with more water in the drum than you need--leaving you with a heavy problem in your pickup bed.

Having some way to determine when you have enough water in the barrel is the trick. We used algebra to determine how many gallons of water were in our barrel, based on the height of the water. Since we can't see through the barrel wall, we used an indelible marker to clearly mark our filler hose with graduated steps.

Now we simply feed the filler hose into the drum, pushing it down to the appropriate level in the barrel. For example, putting it in about two feet will fill the barrel to about 35 gallons. With the hose in the barrel, we fill it until the sound of the in-rushing water changes, signaling that the water has reached the tip of the filler hose.

But how do you get the water out of the barrel and into the RV? The height of our RV water fill inlet was far above the level of our pickup bed. For a couple of years we put the barrel on top of the truck tool box, filled it, and then used gravity to syphon water out of the barrel and into the RV. Hauling the barrel back from the water station was a bit of a nerve wracker, as the barrel threatened to slide off the tool box and smash onto the road.

We finally got an extra 12 volt RV water pump, and use that to pump water out of the barrel and into the rig. Now we can transit the barrel in the pickup bed, and don't fear dropping it. We connect the pump wiring to the battery charge line at the back of the pickup. Of course, this means we have to switch the truck ignition system on to get power to the charge line, but the pump works quickly.

Other Water Toters

Hauling a water drum isn't practical for everyone, particularly if you use a "toad car." A commercial water "bladder," is a vinyl bag that reminds us of a waterbed mattress. The bladder is laid out flat on the roof of the toad car (or a pickup). Others, who tow small station wagons, SUVs, or minivans simply open the back door and lay the bladder out on the cargo area floor.

Back in camp you simply connect your filler hose from roof mounted bladders to the RV inlet port and let gravity fill your tank. If the bladder is lower than the RV's fresh water tank, neither siphoning nor gravity will do--you'll need to add a pump to transfer the precious liquid.

Bladder owners swear by their systems. One gent, who used a large "fruit juice barrel" for a long time made the switch after his barrel jumped off the top of his motorhome and skidded off down the freeway. He says he'd never go back. "It's so much better. Takes up less space, I just roll it up and put it back in the box. I don't have to worry about cleaning it, and it's a lot lighter."

One RVer with an SUV we met has another unique method of hauling fresh water. He located a used fresh water tank at an RV salvage yard. Using 2 x 4 lumber and plywood he constructed a shelf inside over the rear wheel wells, just inside the back door. The "recycled" fresh water tank lies on the shelf. Now he rolls up to the water station, opens his back door and fills the tank. Back at his rig he uses a 12 volt pump to transfer the liquid.

CHAPTER 7

Don't Let Waste Water Get You Down in the Dumps

Like it or not, what goes in, must come out. RVs produce waste water--prodigious amounts of it. Both gray water (the stuff that comes out of sink and shower drains) and black water (from the toilet) have to be disposed of properly.

We say "properly" because law and polite manners certainly dictate that black water be appropriately disposed of--in a sewage treatment system. You'll find too, that most campground overseers also require that gray water be disposed of in the same way.

How do you get your waste water to the dump station? You could hitch up the rig and drive down to the dump station every time you get a full tank. Many motorhome folks do just that. But if you're "dug in" for a long stay in one place, breaking camp just to empty tanks can be a time-wasting experience. Enter the "Blue Boy."

"Blue boys" are portable waste tanks, dubbed that because most commercially made tanks of this nature are built from blue colored plastic. To dump your rig tank, you typically connect a sewer hose to your dump valve, then connect the other end to a fitting on the blue boy. Instead of breaking camp, you simply lug the blue boy to the dump station.

Blue Boy Varieties

There are a couple of different types of portable waste tanks. Most are equipped with a pair of wheels and a "wagon tongue" or draw bar-like apparatus that allows you to tow the tank behind a vehicle using a hitch ball. Once at the station you lift the blue boy, pivoting it on its wheels, dumping the tank through the same port by which you filled it.

Smaller blue boys, say up to 10 gallons, are easily handled. But the bigger the tank, the harder that lifting is. More than one RVer has strained a back lifting the larger blue boys. Another (and more expensive) type of blue boy adds an RV dump valve to the side of the tank. Once towed to the dump station, you hook a sewer hose onto the side valve, pull the handle, and viola! No lifting required!

Regardless of the type of blue boy you use, however, all have their "Achilles heel." Unless you stick solely to camping on paved roads, the wheels on blue boys are notorious for eventually wearing out, or worse, coming off. These little blue guys may look sturdy, but drop a wheel off while towing a tanker load of black water and you're sure to have a *memorable* day. A crushed sidewall or base on a blue boy yields surprisingly smelly results.

Using Blue Boys

Using a blue boy is not a whole lot different than dumping at a dump station with a couple of added details. When filling a blue boy at the rig, do as you would at a dump station: dump your black water *first*, leaving yourself gray water for "rinsing" the hose. Since you probably won't have a ready source of fresh water available for rinsing your dump hose, this makes the order of dumping critical. And since you won't likely have enough blue boy capacity to handle your entire load of black water in one trip, leave just a bit of "head space" in the blue boy to allow for a couple of gallons of gray water for the rinse.

Don't try to economize by dumping your black water tanks early. *Always* have at least three-quarters of a tank of black water prior to dumping, since dumping too early tends to allow for a buildup of solids in the bottom of the holding tank. That spells real trouble after a while, when you reach the point where you can't overcome that buildup and you find yourself stuck with a tankful of ickiness that you can't get rid of.

When dumping holding tanks into the blue boy, we find that the black water tank tends to get a little stubborn about letting go of its secrets. To overcome this problem, after the last of the black water is emptied into the blue boy, we close the black water valve and disconnect the hose from the blue boy. We then lift the free end of the dump hose above the level of the holding tanks. Next we reopen the black water valve, then the gray water valve. This allows gray water to rush from the gray tank into the black water tank. After things "equalize" between the tanks, we close both valves, and reconnect the hose to the blue boy. At this point we reopen the black water valve, allowing the diluted contents to drain into the blue boy.

If you decide to try this, it's important to make sure you have a good "head" of gray water built up. This prevents black water from infiltrating the gray water system, and the goodly amount of gray water will push back into the black water tank for thorough rinsing.

Blue Boy Modifications

While manufacturers always caution you to keep the speed down while towing a blue boy--typically to "no faster than you can walk," it can seem a long way to the dump station. Even before losing a wheel, some RVers make changes to their blue boy carriages.

Some replace the hard rubber "factory" tires on their tanks with pneumatic wheels. Others simply take the wheels off their blue boys, and mount the whole works on a hand truck, like those used for moving light appliances. After gouging the daylights out of our 25 gallon blue boy, we opted for the hand truck trick. We used "aircraft cable" from the hardware store to firmly strap the tank onto a $15 hand truck. The hand truck can be hooked up to a ball hitch either with the factory tongue, or with a simple loop made of strong rope.

All this is great, provided the dump station is located relatively near to your camp site--at least, without having to hit the public road or highway system. But what if you need to haul your blue boy someplace where rolling it on the pavement might be frowned on?

Some RVers have come up with elaborate ramps and pulley hoists to yank their tank onto a pickup bed. Others have constructed a tank platform out of plywood, balanced on a chunk of square steel that fits into their hitch receiver. The platform tilts down to the ground, allowing the blue boy to be rolled on, then tilted up so the tank is suspended on the platform in "travel position." In this way they can "wheel their waste" at highway speed.

A few RVers have discovered that their rigs are so close to the ground that they can't get sufficient slope to drain their holding tanks into their blue boys. If this is your case, your only resort may be to dig a hole in the ground large enough to "drop in" your blue boy. It's best to "ramp" the hole so that pulling out the blue boy is made easier.

In the case of our blue boy, which is a large one with a long draw bar, trying to lift up the draw bar to attach it to the hitch ball was more than we could physically mange. To overcome this, we tied a stout rope onto the draw bar. When the tank is full, we loop the rope over the hitch ball and drive forward until the blue boy is up out of the hole. Then lifting the draw bar to the hitch ball is easy and we're off to the dump station.

Rip and Tear? Repair!

Even folks who are cautious with their blue boys may have the occasional odd problem to deal with. Factory equipped blue boys are notorious for their dislike of rough roads, and if your waste mobile should lose its wheel, all is not lost.

Even nasty gashes in blue boys can be successfully--albeit ugily--repaired. One method is to obtain a rubber patch a couple of inches wider and longer than the damage. We've found that rubber carpet runner (obtained at a hardware store or carpet retailer) makes a great patch. Clean up the damaged area with spray kitchen cleaner and thoroughly clear away any cleaner residue with a damp rag. Apply a thick layer of sealant from the hardware store an inch or so around the margins of the patch.

Stick the patch on the blue boy, and reinforce with sheet metal screws every couple of inches around the margin of the patch. Be sure to allow a good amount of dry time before putting your repaired tank back in service. Done right, it should stop the leak --or at least reduce it significantly.

One RVer we know has at times been able to patch smaller holes in blue boys using similar plastic material and "welding" it into place with a blow torch. He swears by plastic milk jug material, and says that on small (1 or 2 inch in diameter) holes it works well. He heats up the blue boy until it gets somewhat gummy, then quickly lays on a patch cut from the milk jug. He then applies heat to the patch to meld the two materials together.

While this may work for small holes, we can tell you from experience (on trying to "rescue" a cast-off blue boy) that it doesn't work well with long gashes. We wound up with a hole much larger than we started with, and the dumpster wound up with our efforts.

Don't Wait--Macerate!

Other, more elaborate systems might work well for you, if you don't like the blue boy approach. Some RVers modify a closed plastic drum, fitting an RV waste valve into the drum head. Lifting the empty drum onto their pickup bed is easy. Then by using a macerator pump--a 12 volt operated pump that grinds and pumps waste through a garden hose--they fill the tank and haul it off to the dump station.

Using this method may be more expedient for some, as you can carry a lot of waste at one time. Nevertheless, pumping out waste with a macerator can be a time-consuming proposition, and the added power consumption is a factor to consider. If you want to undertake building your own big truck mounted waste tank, here are some tips: Smooth sided drums are best. At least the *inside* of the drum should be smooth, to prevent the buildup of gunk.

Attaching the waste valve to the tank is where individual circumstances dictate construction methods. Perhaps the easiest is when a threaded bung matches a common plastic plumbing coupler. Screw the coupler into the bung, then attach a small waste valve via a flange to the coupler. On the "delivery" side of the waste valve, you'll probably need to use the appropriate adapter to "upsize" to match the size for the bayonet hose coupling needed to attach the rig to a dump hose. If the sizes are different, you may need to go to the hardware store and get creative.

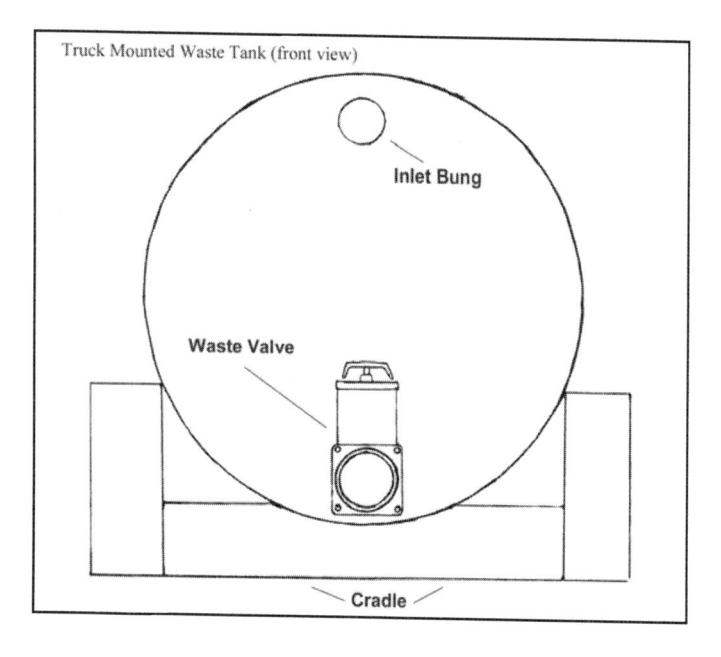

Truck Mounted Waste Tank (front view)

Inlet Bung

Waste Valve

Cradle

Constructing a "cradle" out of 2x6 or larger material, with a custom cut curve to match the outside of the drum will keep the waste hauler from drifting around in the bed of the truck. Note the following diagram for some thinking on the matter.

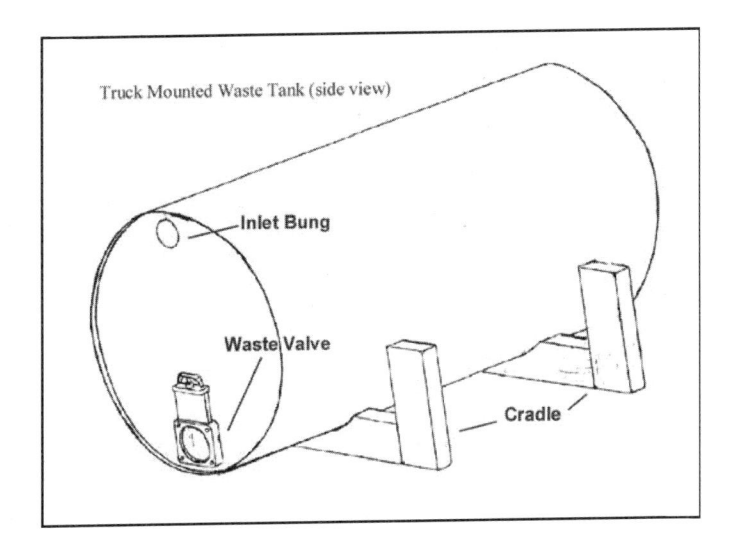

Truck Mounted Waste Tank (side view) — Inlet Bung, Waste Valve, Cradle

Odor Problems

At times, boondockers encounter unusually odoriferous black water problems. This can become particularly pronounced after a long spell of sitting in one place and not moving the rig. Black water problems are the subject of many campfire conversations, and some really weird suggestions tend to surface on how to deal with them.

We do not subscribe to the school of "home brew holding tank chemicals." And many dump stations have banned the use of formaldehyde containing tank chemicals, so we don't use these either. Rather, we use a commercial treatment that is based on bacteria and enzymes, used to break down waste and thoroughly "digest" it.

One season, we were about to start shopping for a new treatment. Our black water tank odors were so rank our ability to hold our breath nearly rivaled that of native pearl divers. Something had to be done, or one or both of us would be moving out. After a couple of conversations with our holding tank treatment manufacturer's chemist, we finally hit on the solution.

First we dumped the black water tank and refilled it nearly to the top with fresh water--to which we added two cups of baking soda. This was allowed to "brew" for a couple of days, after which we dumped the tank and "restarted" the digestion process by adding our holding tank treatment. Away went the stink.

What was the problem? It seems that holding tanks can "sour" when sitting around and stewing for long periods. Adding the baking soda pumped up the oxygen level in the tank, and got things moving along again. When on the road, the action of the black water sloshing around in the tank tends to keep things from going sour, and oxygen is agitated into the mix.

Bottom line: If your tank *really* stinks, it may be it needs a little livening up. Add baking soda, or hitch up and shake things up a bit. Adding a bag of ice cubes to your holding tank before you pull out will also tend to knock loose any "crud" sticking to the sides of the tank. Don't have a full tank if you try this trick-- the ice will simply float on the very top of the tank and not give the appropriate scrubbing action.

CHAPTER 8
Staying Warm Without Losing Your Cool

Even folks who flee the north country and head south for the winter find themselves needing heat from time to time. Don't let anybody fool you, the Desert Southwest may be 'shirt sleeve' weather by day, but winter nights can be down right chilling.

How can you warm up without wiping out your battery bank? There are several ways.

Furnace Follies

The typical RV furnace chews up propane *and* electricity. That's because furnace design is taken from land-based "forced air" systems which heat up the air in an enclosed firebox, circulating cool air over the outside of the firebox, and blasting it out through the rig with a fan.

If you stick your hand near the outside exhaust port of your RV furnace, you'll find quite a bit of heat blasting by--enough to burn your hand. Lots of those little British Thermal Units coming marching out of your firebox, only to contribute to desert warming. A forced air RV furnace isn't all that efficient.

For the boondocker, the real problem is how much electrical power your furnace consumes. Even a small, non-ducted furnace system (like those used in truck campers or pop-ups) can chew up 5 amps of power for every hour of operation. The bigger your rig, the more ducting the air has to be pushed through, and in short order, you can eat up your battery banks overnight.

In our experience, a forced air RV furnace is best used when tied up to shore power, or for short spells to "take the chill off." Where does that leave you for keeping the place warm for extended times?

"Cat" Heaters

While our own four-footed cat thinks our "cat heater" was made just for her, "cat" stands for catalytic. These flameless heaters are the "cat's meow" for producing lots of heat with little or no electrical power consumption.

A catalytic heater uses a specially coated catalyst "bed" or mat to efficiently burn propane. They are "flameless" after lighting--they do produce a bit of a flare when first being started--as our own cat was rue to find out. She stuck her face right up to the heater and it flared, giving her a "close shave," and the loss of a few whiskers. She learned quickly and now stays back several inches anytime we're lighting the thing up.

Catalytic heaters are highly efficient, 95 percent or better of your propane fuel is turned into heat, all of it released inside the rig. Most are small, and can mount directly on a wall, as they have very small clearance areas required. They can also be put on legs (cat feet?) and pointed wherever heat is needed.

Since they are "radiant" heaters, they will quickly warm up any object or person in front of them, but they do take time to 'heat up the house.' This is because the radiant heat of a cat heater has to be absorbed by something (or someone) and then gradually released. Think in terms of walls and floors. However, they are practical for heating your rig.

Catalytic heaters do have their drawbacks: Since they are "non-vented," meaning that they don't release anything to outside of the rig, they will add moisture to your RV air. If you're in an area of high humidity, a cat heater will only add to the dampness. They also draw their air for combustion from inside your rig. The catalytic process requires less oxygen than an open flame, but it is a consideration. It is best to crack a window whenever your run a cat heater, so that the air used can be replaced.

The heart and soul of a catalytic heater is its catalytic "bed" or mat. This specially impregnated material is where all the heating takes place. Susceptible to pollutants, if you frequent areas where air pollution is rampant, the bed won't last as long as it might otherwise. As well, contaminants from propane or propane containers can migrate their way up the propane lines into the catalytic heater contaminating the bed. Our own catalytic heater has had to be sent in for service when guck from the propane lines clogged some fine orifices, reducing the heat output significantly.

What's to be done? Olympian, the maker of a large number of catalytic heaters, makes several recommendations. First, when not in use, catalytic heaters should be kept covered. You can buy specially designed covers from your catalytic heater manufacturer. This tends to keep the airborne pollutants off the cat bed.

As far as fuel-borne contaminants, Olympian recommends avoiding the use of LP produced in Mexico. The company says this fuel often contains contaminants that can clog orifices and damage catalytic beds.

Olympian also recommends that RV propane cylinders be "purged" once a year to remove tank contaminants. This is an operation best performed by an LP dealer. It's not an expensive operation, and with catalytic beds costing in excess of $100 (not to mention labor charges) if you run a catalytic heater, it's cheap insurance.

Some catalytic heaters (as well as some "blue flame" type heaters) have a sensor that detects a low oxygen condition, and will shut themselves down before the oxygen level is so low that it could be harmful to "air breathers" like us. That can be a drawback if you take your rig to higher altitudes--the air being so "thin" at some levels that the cat heater won't work. Be sure to ask your dealer about how high you can travel and still use your heater. Another disclaimer: Be sure to follow the manufacturer's safety information. Try not to become a negative statistic.

Cat heaters are rated based on their heat output, measured in BTUs (there they are again, those British Thermal Units!). The greater the BTU output, the higher the cost, but of course, the larger the area that can be heated.

Most cat heaters use NO electricity. This is great for solar and wind power users--stay warm, while keeping the batteries for other uses. However, these "no power cats" have a drawback: They have no thermostat. Generally, you'll have a choice of "high, medium, or low" output, but if they're on, they're always heating. There are thermostat equipped "cats" that do use a small amount of power to control heat output to keep things more comfortable if the inside temperature fluctuates. Still, we've learned how to put up with the lack of thermostatic control and can usually tell at bedtime at just what setting to leave our cat heater.

Freestanding Flame Heaters

Somewhat related to cat heaters are other "non-vented" heaters that actually produce a flame in operation. The flame is usually shielded behind safety glass, but still visible to the user. It's almost like having your own "fireplace" (assuming you have a fair amount of imagination). Marketed under brand names like "BlueFlame," these heaters generally have a higher heat output than a cat heater.

Many of these flame type heaters have a standing pilot light, that allows the use of a mechanical thermostat. Nice, not having to use power, but still having a steady heat source. Some users leave their flame heaters on all the time, just set to the desired temperature. Others only "fire them up," when things get chilly, saving that small amount of propane by not leaving the pilot lit.

Once again, most of these creatures are non-vented, so they "breath" your inside air. CAREFULLY follow the instructions of the manufacturer about how much you'll need to leave a window open to make sure you wake up the next morning. As was mentioned earlier, some of these heaters are equipped with oxygen sensors that may play havoc with your heat availability when traveling in higher altitudes. Some RVers have been known to try and defeat these sensors, but we DO NOT RECOMMEND IT. We'd like to keep you around to buy our next book!

"Brick" Heaters

Not as "cute" as a flame heater, but costing less than a catalytic heater comes the so-called "brick heater." These heaters use a ceramic "brick" with tiny orifices as a heat source. Some have adjustable thermostats for "perfect control," while others (cheaper) allow you to set the heat output, and live with it until you readjust it.

Like cats and flame heaters, they too, draw inside air for combustion. The same safety precautions apply.

Heater Plumbing

Since cats, flame type, and brick heaters all require propane to fire, you have to get the propane into them some way. *Here's another disclaimer*: Be sure to follow all local, state, and federal applicable laws and codes when installing auxiliary heat systems in your RV. Check with your heater dealer about facts on these matters.

Some folks use copper tubing to "tie into" the RV propane system, leaving the heater right where it's mounted. Others find that using the appropriate rubber tubing allows them to "point" their heater or move it where needed. Some even use "quick connect" fittings to allow them to disconnect the heater and move it to another place in the RV.

Other Stay Warm Tricks

There are other alternatives and ideas to help you stay warm on chilly days. First, never underestimate the power of a sweater, and in really bitter cold snaps, sleeping with a stocking hat on.

Orientation of your rig can also do wonders for absorbing available solar energy. If you direct the broad side of the rig to the east, you'll pick up the heat of the morning sun and absorb it. One boondocker we know has "summer" and "winter" orientation angles figured out. He places the largest surface area of his rig pointed toward the east and south in winter, but when the days get warmer, he reorients so his rig takes the least amount of sun exposure.

How about using the range top or oven for a little spare heat? This is not something we advocate or recommend. Using cooking appliances to heat the enclosed space of an RV can prove hazardous to your health. Of course, trying to cook on your cat heater can prove hazardous to your food. It isn't so great for the heater, either.

CHAPTER 9
On the Other Hand: Hot Ideas for Staying Cool

While some boondockers have gensets to power up those large appliances, it isn't always necessary to bring up the "Onan Chorus" when the sun stands high above the old RV roof. Solar and wind "purists" also stay out of the heat with success.

Make Your Shade

Shade is the boondocker's best friend for keeping cool. Of course, using shade has to be balanced against the needs of solar panels, and too much shade can spell wind turbine interruptions from turbulence created by trees. However, you can often provide your own shade through rig orientation and use of awnings.

By presenting the least amount of rig sidewall to the hot sun, Sol has less opportunity to overheat your rig. Hence, orienting the front or rear side of the rig to the south can help. But which end? Determine which side of the rig would get the "worst" of the sun's heat, and orient so that your awning rolls out to protect that side. Adding a shade cloth to the awning can provide a nice area to retreat to when things get too hot inside.

While many newer rigs are equipped white rubber roofs, those owning older rigs may find it beneficial to paint a coat of white reflecting coating up topside.

We've found that putting insulated padding in non-openable windows really cuts down heat infiltration. The stuff is sold by the foot and can be cut with scissors to match window sizes. We identify ours for reuse by writing on the pad with an indelible marker. Putting aluminum foil on window louvers cuts down heat infiltration while still allowing a free flow of air.

Mechanical Marvels

Refrigerated air conditioning systems aren't the only mechanical ways of keeping the heat down. Low voltage "swamp coolers" designed for RVs can also make life a lot more tolerable in hot, dry climates. They aren't much use when the humidity is up, but in more arid areas, a swamp cooler provides favorable results without the high energy consumption of refrigerated air conditioner units.

Just getting the hot air "out" of the rig can do wonders. A roof vent equipped with a fan can pump out hot air quickly. Even easier are automatic roof vents such as "Fan-Tastic" ceiling fans which have thermostats that automatically respond to inside temperatures and switch on to ventilate. Fancy ones even have a system that responds to rain, shutting the vent to protect you from wet.

CHAPTER 10

Boondockers' Conservation Tips

Successful boondocking means getting beyond the technical "nuts and bolts," and put into practice measures that allow you to stay out in the boonies longer. There's a bit of a conservation "ethic" involved. Here are a few tips from successful boondockers.

Kitchen and Bath

Wasted water hurts two ways--depleting fresh water resources and filling up holding tanks. Cut down wherever possible.

Brushing teeth? Don't leave the tap on while scrubbing your molars. Turn off the tap and use it only when rinsing.

The same applies to scrubbing the rest of your epidermis. Think "Navy Shower," where you'll turn off the shower water while "soaping up." Most RV showers have a valve that allows the water flow to be turned off at the shower head, so there's no hassle to reset the hot and cold water mixture. Take advantage of it.

"No water" car wash products applied to shower stall walls (not the floor!) makes water and soap film roll off. This cuts the amount of water and effort to keep the shower clean.

It doesn't take an ocean to flush the toilet. Pump a little fresh water in the bowl before dumping its contents. A spray bottle of water with a touch of soap helps too.

Reduce dishwashing needs through dishware conservation. Try keeping the same cup or glass throughout the day. Some boondockers find paper plates a great saver--they reduce dish washing and provide fodder for starting campfires.

Try limiting dishwashing to once per day. And instead of washing dishes in the sink, reduce water consumption by using a dish tub in the sink. It reduces the overall amount of water used.

"Pre-wipe" dishes instead of "pre-rinsing." Using a little toilet paper to get rid of the grunge will save a lot of water and effort in the sink.

We save our dish *rinse* water. Instead of dumping it down the drain, we save it outside the rig in a covered bucket. Our potted plants love it. We don't have to haul fresh water for the plants, nor take out "light gray water" to the dump station.

Consider using the barbecue more often. It cuts down on cookware and inside mess. Tastes great too!

We conserve space and economize too, by making use cleaning products that do more than one job. For example, we use vinegar and water for floor cleaning instead of special floor cleaners.

And Those Clothes?

Keeping the body clean while conserving water and power is one thing, getting the clothes washed can be quite another. Yes, we know there are folks who actually have a washer/dryer in their RV. If you don't have one, and are thinking about one, consider this:

The typical RV washer/dryer operates on 120 volt shore power. It takes A LOT of power to operate either side of these characters, and the most common complaint about them--even when used in RV parks--is, "It takes forever to dry clothes!"

We tried an alternative in our travels, a "portable clothes washer," touted far and wide in RV catalogs. The rig looks like a small drum, held up in a frame, with a handle that allows you to provide the mechanical power to "agitate" your clothes clean. We figured, "Shucks, it only costs $35, how can we go wrong?" It took but one session with the little wonder to find out the answer to that question.

The portable unit did somewhat clean the clothes. However, to adequately rinse them it took far more water than we ever anticipated. But the end result, even if somewhat clean, was a wet, sopping mess. Trying to wring out those jeans prior to drying was a task best left to Sampson. We sold our "portable washer" a few weeks later to somebody with more ambition.

We've found it best to simply surrender to a trip into town, where we use commercial washers in the Laundromat. We bring the clean, wet clothing home and hang it to dry. Where? Our next door neighbor actually plants a laundry drying rack on her site, and allows us to use it. The rig is a single pole, on top of which is a clever frame that allows you to hang many yards of laundry in a area covering about eight feet square.

Recognizing not everybody wants to store, set up, and tear down such an apparatus, we have another alternative that we've used many times with success. We roll out our RV awning, and then string clothes line between the awning arms. It's not difficult, and about three runs of line between the arms handles our biggest wash day. We do dry our "permanent press" clothes at the Laundromat to prevent wrinkling, although if you have a fairly stiff wind, you can often 'get away' with drying these on the line. Because we hang dry, we use liquid fabric softener in our wash loads.

More Power to You

Fluorescent lights produce more light with less power than do incandescent lights.

We've installed an LP powered mantle lamp above our kitchen table. It produces copious amounts of light without drawing down the batteries. It also takes the chill off the room on a cool night. We make sure we have enough ventilation when operating it.

If you have a tendency to fall asleep while watching television, use the "timer" function shut it off when you might nod off.

Don't use lights for decoration, but rather, for work. Turn off lights not actually being used.

"Porch lights" attract bugs and eat up a lot of juice with little benefit. If you really want bright outdoor light, consider getting a small "plug into the cigarette lighter" power inverter. Plug it into your tow vehicle, then to a lamp fixture equipped with a power-conserving light bulb. The output is great, and the power consumption is very low.

We keep a "spare" deep cycle battery handy. We've rigged special wiring to use it to power our 12 volt television, while keeping the battery outside the coach. When the battery level gets low, we hook it to our tow vehicle's "charge wire" and recharge it when running errands.

Hot and Cold Running People?

When the chill sets in, don't automatically turn up the thermostat. Putting on a sweater may make burning extra LP unnecessary.

Orient your rig to take advantage of the sun on the broad side of the rig in winter. In summer, reorient to reduce sun exposure and keep the rig cooler. Rolling out the awning to keep the rig shaded will reduce inside temperatures.

Use the roof vents to make for effective cooling. Adjust windows and roof vents before trying cooling fans.

If your refrigerator can't keep up with hot summer temperatures, try to keep the cooler's outside panel out of the direct sun. A small, low voltage "muffin fan" oriented to blow air upward over the cooling unit fins will make it chill more efficiently. Be sure to shut the fan off at night to conserve power.

These same muffin fans can help move air around your rig when heating with a "cat" or "blue flame" heater. They use a lot less power than the fans in your furnace and may be enough to keep you from having to fire the furnace.

APPENDIX

Source Guide

Batteries:

Rolls Batteries
(978) 745-3333   www.rollsbattery.com

Optima Batteries
(888) 867-8462 or (303) 340-4550
www.optimabatteries.com

Trojan Batteries
www.trojanbattery.com

Inverters:

There are several "branded" inverter products. An internet search under "RV power inverter" will yield many results.

Solar Panels

BP Solar
(410) 981-0240 www.bpsolar.com

Kyocera Solar, Inc.
(800) 544-6466 or (480) 948-8003
www.kyocerasolar.com

Shell Solar Industries
(805) 48206800
www.shell.com/home/framework?siteId=shellsolar

Wind Turbines

Southwest Windpower
(928) 779-9463 www.windenergy.com

A

amp-hour capacity
  batteries, 12, 20
amps, 10

B

barrels
  water, 61, 62
  water, calculating level, 62
batteries, 17
  amp-hour capacity, 12, 20
  caps, 28
  CCA rating, 19
  checking state of charge, 30
  construction, 18
  deep cycle types, 21
  distilled water, 28
  gell cell, 22
  golf cart, 24
  half-discharge rule, 20
  inverters, 58
  life expectancy, 30
  maintenance, 28
  MCA rating, 19
  Optima, 23
  parallel wiring, 24, 26
  purchasing factors, 25
  reserve capacity, 20
  Rolls, 24
  safety, 22, 26
  series wiring, 27
  series-parallel wiring, 27
  SLI, 17
  solar panel requirements, 36
  state of charge, 30
  twice daily consumption rule, 19
  ventilation, 22
  warranties, 25
  water consumption, 29
battery
  state of charge chart, 31
battery bank requirements
  inverters, 58
battery charging
  inverters, 57
blue boys, 69
  hand truck modification, 67
  ramps, 68
  repairing damage, 68
  rig height problems, 68
BP Solar, 88
brick heaters
  heating systems, 78

C

cat heaters
  cover when not used, 75
  efficiency, 74
  heating systems, 77
  LP from Mexico, 76
  oxygen sensors, 76

purge propane containers, 76
safety considerations, 76
subject to contaminants, 75
catalytic heaters
see cat heaters, 77
CCA rating
batteries, 19
checking state of charge
batteries, 30
clothes cleaning, 84
drying, 84
drying on awning arms, 85
electric dryer power consumption, 84
portable clothes washer, 84
conservation
clothes cleaning, 84
heat, 86
kitchen and bath, 83
LP lighting, 85
water, 83
converters
affect on inverters, 60
cooling, 80
insulate windows, 81
make shade, 80
rig orientation, 80
roof fans, 81
roof reflectance, 81
swamp coolers, 81

cooling fans
refrigerator, 86
current consumption chart, 15
cut-in speed
wind turbines, 48

D

deep cycle batteries
types of, 21
digital multimeter, 30
diodes
solar panels, 42
distilled water
batteries, 28
dynamic braking
wind turbines, 49

F

furnaces
heating systems, 70, 74
power consumption, 74

G

gell cell
batteries, 22
golf cart
batteries, 24

H

half-discharge rule
batteries, 20
hand truck modification

blue boys, 67
heat
   conservation, 86
heating systems
   add a fan, 86
   brick heaters, 78
   cat heaters, 77
   free standing flame heaters, 77
   furnace power consumption, 74
   furnaces, 70, 74
   plumbing, 78
holding tank chemicals
   waste water, 71

I

inverter, 13
   inefficiencies, 13
inverters
   batteries, 58
   battery bank requirements, 58
   battery charging, 57
   defined, 56
   disconnect refrigerator, 60
   explosive atmosphere, 59
   inefficiency, 58
   installation, 60
   modified sine wave, 56
   remote control, 57
   selection, 57
   sizing, 57
   standby current draw, 57
   suppliers, 87
   true sine wave, 57
   turn off power converter, 60

K

kitchen and bath
   conservation, 83
Kyocera Solar, 88

L

life expectancy
   batteries, 30
lightening safety
   wind turbines, 54
longevity
   solar panels, 35

M

macerators
   waste water, 70
maintenance
   batteries, 28
   solar panels, 43
maximum wind rating
   wind turbines, 49
MCA rating
   batteries, 19
modified sine wave
   inverters, 56

N

noise
    wind turbines, 46

O

Optima
    batteries, 23
Optima Batteries, 87

P

parallel wiring
    batteries, 24, 26
peak output
    wind turbines, 47
power consumption
    shore power equipment, 13
power consumption worksheet, 11
propane
    contaminants, 76

R

ramps
    blue boys, 68
rated output
    wind turbines, 46
refrigerator
    cooling fans, 86
    during inverter use, 60
reserve capacity
    batteries, 20
Rolls batteries, 24, 87

roof fans
    cooling, 81

S

safety
    batteries, 26
    wind turbines, 51, 53
series wiring
    batteries, 27
series-parallel wiring
    batteries, 27
Shell Solar Industries, 88
shore power equipment
    power consumption, 13
Siemens Solar Industries, 88
solar panels
    cost, 35
    diodes, 42
    expected output, 36
    installation, 43
    longevity, 35
    maintenance, 43
    sizing system requirements, 36
    temperature affects, 38
    tilt chart, 38
    tilt system designs, 39
    tilting, 37
    types of, 36
    voltage regulator, 42
Southwest Windpower, 88
standby current draw
    inverters, 57
state of charge

batteries, 30
state of charge chart
   battery, 31
static electricity
   wind turbines, 54
swamp coolers
   cooling, 81
swept area
   wind turbines, 48

T

telescoping mast system
   wind turbines, 52
tilt chart
   solar panels, 38
tilting
   solar panels, 37
tower top weight
   wind turbines, 50
towers
   wind turbines, 53
Trojan Batteries, 87
true sine wave
   inverters, 57

V

voltage regulator
   solar panels, 42

W

warranties
   batteries, 25
waste water

holding tank chemicals, 71
macerators, 70
odors, 71
proper disposal, 64
truck mounted tank designs, 70
water
   barrels, 62
   barrels, gravity feed, 62
   conservation, 83
   recycled water tanks, 63
water consumption
   batteries, 29
watt-hours, 13
wind turbines
   avoiding turbulence, 51
   blade materials, 48
   comparing, 47
   cost, 45
   cut-in speed, 48
   dynamic braking, 49
   freestanding, 53
   governing & regulation, 50
   lightening safety, 54
   maximum wind rating, 49
   noise, 46, 50
   operation and maintenance, 55
   output varies by terrain, 44
   peak output, 47

rated output, 46
safety, 51, 53
shut down methods, 50
sizing the system, 46
static electricity, 54
swept area, 48
telescoping mast system, 52
tower top weight, 50
towers, 53
voltage output, 48
wind speed to power output, 47
wiring, 54

Notes

We Hope You've Enjoyed

RV Boondocking Basics
A Guide to Living Without Hookups

Additional copies of this book are available by mail. Please call or write for the latest edition and price information.

We're always working on new projects to support the RV lifestyle--and new books are "in the works." If you'd like to be notified when new books for the RVer are published, please fill out the coupon below and mail it in. We never sell your name or address information to anyone!

ICanRV Publishing 1910 E. 4th #119 Olympia, WA 98506
Phone: (360) 357-5728   E mail: info@icanrv.com

Please notify me when new books of interest to RVers are published

Name_____

Address_____

City_____State_____ Zip Code_____

E-mail Address:_____